Essays of Shakespeare

ESSAYS OF

Shakespeare

AN ARRANGEMENT
BY

George Coffin Taylor

Essay Index Reprint Series

BOOKS FOR LIBRARIES PRESS
FREEPORT, NEW YORK

INTERNATIONAL STANDARD BOOK NUMBER:
0-8369-2174-7

LIBRARY OF CONGRESS CATALOG CARD NUMBER:
73-134133

PRINTED IN THE UNITED STATES OF AMERICA

Essay Titles

➤➤《《《‐

[v]

[vi]

Introduction

->>><<<-

It is universally acknowledged that Shakespeare was a great poet and dramatist. But many great minds have denied him a place in their own group. This has given rise to the belief that Shakespeare was lacking in intellect, philosophy, ideas, and opinions. "Shakespeare," says Mark Van Doren, "has been denied mentality."

The list of Shakespearean detractors is long and impressive. Critics of reputation and of supposedly good taste have given credence to the idea that the gods gave perhaps their most wonderful power of expression to one lacking in high mentality. Voltaire, Napoleon, and Tolstoi considered his plays pitiful. In our own day, Santayana in his *Three Philosophical Poets* and Osgood in his *The Humanities as a Means of Grace* include Lucretius, Dante, Goethe, Spenser, Milton, even Samuel Johnson in their catalogue of the great. Shakespeare's name is conspicuously absent. Osgood explains why: Shakespeare reflects thought in his works but does not commit himself on the fundamental controversial issues of all time.

Some of the other present-day critics contribute criticisms very adverse. McKail, undisputed authority on Shakespeare in England, says: "But to read a philosophy into Shakespeare, or to invent some 'obsession' in him and hunt for traces of it throughout his work, is not only idle but hurtful. . . . Common sense rejects the more extravagant fancy that Shakespeare embodies . . . a system of human nature and a directory for human life. . . . Shakespeare does not teach; he illuminates." T. S. Eliot, in certain circles a name to conjure with, writes: "I once affirmed that Dante made great poetry out of a great philosophy of life; and that Shakespeare made equally great poetry out of an inferior and muddled philosophy of life. . . . And that when a poet like Shakespeare, who has no 'philosophy' and apparently no design upon the amelioration of our behaviour, sets forth his experience and reading of life, he is forthwith saddled with a 'philosophy' of his own and some esoteric hints towards conduct." And Draper, the most industrious publisher of Shakespeare articles in America, is of the opinion that "Shakespeare regarded philosophy not only with disfavor but with derision and contempt."

There are, to be sure, great thinkers who hold an opinion exactly the reverse. Two of the most respected may serve. Emerson classes Shakespeare as the greatest of all thinkers: "So far from Shakespeare's being the least known, he is the one person, in all modern history, known to us. What point of morals, of manners, of economy, of philosophy, of religion, of taste, of the conduct of life, has he not settled? What mystery has he not signified his knowledge of? What office, or function, or district of man's work, has he not remembered? What king has he not taught state, as Talma taught Napoleon?" Coleridge, regarded by many as the most illuminating of all modern critics, says: "In all the successive courses of lectures delivered by me since my first attempt at the Royal Institution, it has been, and it still remains, my objective, to prove that in all points from the most important to the most minute, the judgment of Shakespeare is commensurate with his genius—nay, that his genius reveals itself in his judgment, as in its most exalted form. . . . Does God choose idiots by whom to convey divine truths to man?"

Why this amazing diversity of opinion? The answer is not far to seek. We cannot be sure that any particular idea in any of Shakespeare's plays or poems reflects his personal opinion or belief as to any controversial matter. That the idea in passing through his mind received a marvelous literary perfection of form is all we can be sure of. In estimating Shakespeare as a thinker among thinkers one must keep in mind the disadvantages which the dramatic form imposes when compared with the essay form in which thinkers or philosophers, so called, traditionally cast their material. By the very nature of his dramatic medium, Shakespeare had to smash every great idea into bits, each of which he then had to stick into the mouths of various characters of high and low degree, and often in a musical form, highly disturbing to reason. Thus, "great thinkers" have a tremendous advantage over Shakespeare with all readers, and Shakespeare's ideas on the themes most dear to essayists, though often more penetrating than theirs, are generally disorganized. Except in his sonnets or in his nondramatic poems, and in a few long digressions, such as Hamlet's discussion of the art of acting, or

Ulysses' discussion of the necessity for a high degree of regimentation in a country involved in war, or Falstaff's discussion of the helpful effect of alcohol on our highest intellectual faculties, Shakespeare is compelled to break his thought into splinters and let it emerge in small units from his various characters. The bits of thought on a certain theme appear, as it were miles apart. Thus scattered, they bring to mind Milton's myth of the body of Osiris, symbolizing Truth, cut into a thousand bits and scattered to the four winds.

It has been my task in this book to gather these scattered fragments and splice them together. Like Milton's friends of Truth who "go up and down gathering up limb by limb," I have endeavored to collect Shakespeare's thoughts on various essay subjects from all his works and put them together in a coherent and logical order in prose form, preserving always however, his exact words.

Readers most familiar with the essays of Bacon and Montaigne realize that they consist in great part of observations on some single theme such as Death, or Ambition, or Truth, very loosely thrown together. It seems only reasonable to put Shakespeare's observations on these same themes together in order that his mentality may be justly estimated in comparison with theirs. When thus collected and fitted together, the developed thoughts of Shakespeare, even if considered as merely incidental to his greatest faculties as artist and dramatist, compare favorably with these same thoughts as developed by the leading thinkers of any period, past or present. Fortunately for us all, the gods at Shake-

speare's birth suspended for a moment the most dia-
bolic of the tragic ironies in which they delight at times:
their grim joke of endowing with supremely great artis-
tic expression persons who have nothing helpful to say
to mankind. Their irony in the case of Cassandra,
blessed with the gift of prophecy, damned with the
curse that no one would hearken to her divine truths,
is trifling compared with this, the greatest of all ironies.
They suspended their irony and gave to Shakespeare
the supreme gift of expressing splendidly splendid
thoughts.

Before we turn to the essays themselves, it is only
fair to admit that objections have come from many
quarters to presenting Shakespeare in any form other
than that intended by him personally. A friend of mine
recently remarked: "We New Yorkers prefer our whisky
and our Shakespeare straight." As to the first I have no
answer; as to getting Shakespeare straight, it is doubtful whether anyone has ever succeeded in doing so since
his plays were acted in his own lifetime. Even then his
actors ad-libbed, improvised, extemporized, and some
of this is still imbedded in his printed material. His
plays were cut and subjected to insertions both by him
and others. During the Commonwealth period portions
of them were "bootlegged." During the seventeenth and
eighteenth centuries they were adapted, changed to
opera. *Lear* with a happy ending held the stage for a
hundred years. In our own time he is modern-dressed,
cut to the bone, radioed, presented through loud-speak-
ers and on movable stages to thousands. Miss Webster
shifts Prospero's most celebrated lines to the epilogue.

From Moscow comes a strapping, robust Ophelia who is rip-roaring drunk and shorn completely of her delicacy and tenderness; and a Hamlet really mad, dying a madman's death. In the face of these adaptations, how can anyone object to presenting Shakespeare in essay form, a form which enables us to estimate his value as a thinker better, perhaps, than any ever devised?

And to enlarge the circle of Shakespeare's readers by any legitimate scheme is to make sure that civilization in common sense will be kept alive.

The Key at the end of the book will be found to be invaluable both for the curious and for "spotters" who may wish to test their memory as they read the essays. Each quotation is identified specifically as to play or poem, act, scene, and line. The Key is based on G. L. Kittredge's *Complete Works of Shakespeare*. Other texts, however, except those which are bowdlerized, may be used.

Thanks must be given to Donald Stauffer, Harlan Hatcher, Frank Dobie, Carl Van Doren, Barbara Henderson, Louis Graves, Heyward Gibbes, Robert Beverly Herbert, Edgar W. Knight, Earle Balch, and Richard G. Sheehan for becoming excited over these essays when they were in their various stages of development. Their enthusiasm contributed immensely to my being disposed to bring to a conclusion the almost endless and exacting task of weaving these thousands of separated sentences together cohesively. Thanks, too, I must give to Miss Caroline Pace, once my student, now a professor at the

Florida College for Women, who first aided me in bringing together expressions in Shakespeare's work which had too long been separated from one another. The initial suggestion for this book came to me forty-four years ago as I walked across the campus of the University of Colorado with my friend Melancthon Libby, when he said to me, "With your memory, why don't you throw together Shakespeare's scattered observations in such fashion as to show that Shakespeare could have written, had he cared, better essays than Francis Bacon?" The idea of preserving Shakespeare's text in exact form, but printing it as prose in order that his ideas should stand out with less intensity but with greater clearness, came to me only comparatively recently. Thus Shakespeare may reach at last those thousands of readers so constituted by nature as to dislike the looks of those pages in any book which look out upon us in the form of poetry. It is my hope that it may prove a way of bringing Shakespeare back to the people, and thus another method of keeping civilization alive.

GEORGE COFFIN TAYLOR

Chapel Hill
April 16, 1947

Essays of Shakespeare

Of Truth

-»>-«-

How this world is given to lying! Truth's a dog must
to kennel; he must be whipp'd out, when Lady the
brach may stand by th' fire and stink. There is scarce
truth enough alive to make societies secure, but security
enough to make fellowships accurst.

What authority and show of truth can cunning sin
cover itself withal! So may the outward shows be least
themselves; the world is still deceiv'd with ornament.
In law, what plea so tainted and corrupt but, being
season'd with a gracious voice, obscures the show of
evil? In religion, what damned error but some sober
brow will bless it, and approve it with a text, hiding the
grossness with fair ornament? There is no vice so simple
but assumes some mark of virtue on his outward parts.
How many cowards, whose hearts are all as false as stairs
of sand, wear yet upon their chins the beards of Hercules
and frowning Mars; who, inward search'd, have livers
white as milk! And these assume but valour's excrement
to render them redoubted. Thus ornament is but the
guiled shore to a most dangerous sea; the beauteous
scarf veiling an Indian beauty; in a word, the seeming
truth which cunning times put on to entrap the wisest.

The devil can cite Scripture for his purpose. An evil
soul, producing holy witness, is like a villain with a

smiling cheek, a goodly apple rotten at the heart. O, what a goodly outside falsehood hath! And oftentimes, to win us to our harm, the instruments of darkness tell us truths, win us with honest trifles, to betray's in deepest consequence.

If circumstances lead me, I will find where truth is hid, though it were hid indeed within the centre, for truth can never be confirm'd enough, though doubts did ever sleep. This is all true as it is strange. Nay, it is ten times true, for truth is truth to th' end of reck'ning. The truth should live from age to age ... even to the general all-ending day. Who tells me true, though in his tale lie death, I hear him as he flatter'd.

Of Time

>>><<<

TIME travels in divers paces with divers persons. I'll tell you who Time ambles withal, who Time trots withal, who Time gallops withal, and who he stands still withal. . . . He trots hard with a young maid between the contract of her marriage and the day it is solemniz'd. If the interim be but a se'nnight, Time's pace is so hard that it seems the length of seven year. Who ambles Time withal? With a priest that lacks Latin and a rich man that hath not the gout; for the one sleeps easily because he cannot study, and the other lives merrily because he feels no pain; the one lacking the burthen of lean and wasteful learning, the other knowing no burthen of heavy tedious penury. These Time ambles withal. Who doth he gallop withal? With a thief to the gallows; for though he go as softly as foot can fall, he thinks himself too soon there. Who stays it withal? With lawyers in the vacation; for they sleep between term and term, and then they perceive not how Time moves.

Time hath . . . a wallet at his back, wherein he puts alms for oblivion, a great-siz'd monster of ingratitudes. Those scraps are good deeds past, which are devour'd as fast as they are made, forgot as soon as done. Perseverance . . . keeps honour bright. To have done is to hang quite out of fashion, like a rusty mail in monumental mock'ry. Let not virtue seek remuneration for the thing it was! What they do in present, though less than yours in past, must o'ertop yours; for Time is like a fashionable host, that slightly shakes his parting guest by th' hand, and with his arms outstretch'd as he would fly grasps in the comer.... Welcome ever smiles, and farewell goes out sighing. One touch of nature makes the whole world kin, that all with one consent praise new-born gauds, though they are made and moulded of things past, and give to dust that is a little gilt more laud than gilt o'erdusted. The present eye praises the present object.

Have you not heard ... that Time comes stealing on by night and day, reckoning Time; whose million'd accidents creep in 'twixt vows and change decrees of kings, tan sacred beauty, blunt the sharp'st intents, divert strong minds to th' course of alt'ring things. Devouring Time that gave doth now his gift confound ... doth transfix the flourish set on youth and delves the parallels in beauty's brow, feeds on the rarities of nature's truth and nothing stands but for his scythe to mow; beauty, wit, high birth, vigour of bone, desert in service, love, friendship, charity are subjects all to envious and calumniating Time. Do whate'er thou wilt, swift-footed Time, to the wide world and all her fading sweets.... Do thy worst, old Time.

Misshapen Time, sluttish Time, copesmate of ugly Night, swift subtle post, carrier of grisly care, eater of youth, false slave to false delight, base watch of woes, sin's packhorse, virtue's snare! thou nursest all, and

[6]

murth'rest all that are. . . . Why hath thy servant Opportunity betray'd the hours thou gav'st me to repose? Cancell'd my fortunes, and enchained me to endless date of never-ending woes? . . . Time's glory is . . . to fill with wormholes stately monuments, to feed oblivion with decay of things, to blot old books and alter their contents, to pluck the quills from ancient ravens' wings, to dry the old oak's sap and cherish springs, to spoil antiquities of hammer'd steel and turn the giddy round of Fortune's wheel. . . . Why works't thou mischief in thy pilgrimage, unless thou couldst return to make amends? One poor retiring minute in an age would purchase thee a thousand thousand friends.

Time is the nurse and breeder of all good. Every time serves for the matter that is born in't, the baby finger of the giant mass of things to come. Time and the hour runs through the roughest day. Time shall unfold what plighted cunning hides. Time's glory . . . is to make the child a man, the man a child, to slay the tiger that doth live by slaughter, . . . to mock the subtle in themselves beguil'd, to cheer the ploughman with increasful crops, to calm contending kings, to fine the hate of foes, to eat up errors by opinion bred, to unmask falsehood and bring truth to light, to stamp the seal of time in aged things, to wake the morn and sentinel the night, to wrong the wronger till he render right. Whereby I see that Time's the king of men; he's both their parent, and he is their grave, and gives them what he will. The end crowns all, and that old common arbitrator, Time, will one day end it.

Flux or Mutability

→≫≪←

THAT one might read the book of fate, and see the revolution of the times make mountains level, and the continent, weary of solid firmness, melt itself into the sea! and other times to see the beachy girdle of the ocean too wide for Neptune's hips; how chances mock, and changes fill the cup of alteration with divers liquors! O, if this were seen, the happiest youth, viewing his progress through, what perils past, what crosses to ensue, would shut the book and sit him down and die. All that lives must die, passing through nature to eternity. We fat all creatures else to fat us, and we fat ourselves for maggots. Your fat king and your lean beggar is but variable service—two dishes, but to one table. That's the end. . . . A man may fish with the worm that hath eat of a king, and eat of the fish that hath fed of that worm. . . . A king may go a progress through the guts of a beggar.

To what base uses we may return. . . . Why may not imagination trace the noble dust of Alexander till he find it stopping a bunghole? . . . Alexander dies, Alexander was buried, Alexander returneth into dust; the dust is earth; of earth we make loam; and why of that loam (whereto he was converted) might they not stop a beer barrel? Imperious Caesar, dead and turn'd to clay, might stop a hole to keep the wind away.

Great princes' favourites their fair leaves spread but as the marigold at the sun's eye; and in themselves their pride lies buried, for at a frown they in their glory die. The painful warrior famoused for fight, after a thousand victories once foil'd, is from the book of honour rased quite, and all the rest forgot for which he toil'd. Like as the waves make towards the pebbled shore, so do our minutes hasten to their end; each changing place with that which goes before, in sequent toil all forwards do contend. Nativity, once in the main of light, crawls to maturity, wherewith being crown'd, crooked eclipses 'gainst his glory fight.

When I consider every thing that grows holds in perfection but a little moment, that this huge stage presenteth naught but shows whereon the stars in secret influence comment; when I perceive that men as plants increase, cheered and check'd even by the selfsame sky, vaunt in their youthful sap, at height decrease, and wear their brave state out of memory, when I have seen by Time's fell hand defaced the rich proud cost of outworn buried age; when sometime lofty towers I see down-raz'd, and brass eternal slave to mortal rage; when I have seen the hungry ocean gain advantage on the kingdom of the shore, and the firm soil win of the watery main, increasing store with loss, and loss with store; when I have seen such interchange of state, or state itself confounded to decay; ruin hath taught me thus to ruminate, that Time will come and take my love away.

What strong hand can hold his swift foot back? The cloud-capp'd towers, the gorgeous palaces, the solemn temples, the great globe itself, yea, all which it inherit, shall dissolve, and, like this insubstantial pageant faded, leave not a rack behind. This great world shall so wear out to naught.

Of Love

-»>«<-

I do much wonder that one man, seeing how much another man is a fool when he dedicates his behaviours to
love, will, after he hath laugh'd at such shallow follies in
others, become the argument of his own scorn by falling in love. I will not be sworn but love may transform
me to an oyster; but I'll take my oath on it, till he have
made an oyster of me he shall never make me such
a fool.

Love is a smoke rais'd with the fume of sighs; being
purg'd, a fire sparkling in lovers' eyes; being vex'd, a
sea nourish'd with lovers' tears. What is it else? A madness most discreet, a choaking gall, and a preserving
sweet. As in the sweetest bud the eating canker dwells,
so eating love inhabits in the finest wits of all. . . . As
the most forward bud is eaten by the canker ere it blow,
even so by love the young and tender wit is turn'd to
folly. Love is your master, for he masters you; and he
that is so yoked by a fool, methinks should not be
chronicled for wise.

Love is full of unbefitting strains, all wanton as a
child, skipping and vain, form'd by the eye and therefore, like the eye, full of strange shapes, of habits, and
of forms. It is to be all made of fantasy, all made of
passion, and all made of wishes, all adoration, duty, and

observance, all humbleness, all patience, and impatience, all purity, all trial, all obedience. There lives within the very flame of love a kind of wick or snuff that will abate it; and nothing is at a like goodness still; for goodness, growing to a plurisy, dies in his own too-much. Men have died from time to time, and worms have eaten them, but not for love.

Things base and vile, holding no quantity, love can transpose to form and dignity. Love looks not with the eyes, but with the mind. It adds a precious seeing to the eye: a lover's eyes will gaze an eagle blind. A lover's ear will hear the lowest sound when the suspicious head of the theft is stopp'd. Love's feeling is more soft and sensible than are the tender horns of cockled snails. Love's tongue proves dainty Bacchus gross in taste. For valour, is not Love a Hercules, still climbing trees in the Hesperides? Subtle as Sphinx; as sweet and musical as bright Apollo's lute, strung with his hair. And when Love speaks, the voice of all the gods make heaven drowsy with the harmony. Never durst poet touch a pen to write until his ink were temper'd with Love's sighs.... Then his lines would ravish savage ears and plant in tyrants mild humility.

Let me not to the marriage of true minds admit impediments. Love is not love which alters when it alteration finds or bends with the remover to remove. O, no! it is an ever-fixed mark that looks on tempests and is never shaken; it is the star to every wand'ring bark, whose worth's unknown, although his highth be taken. Love's not Time's fool, though rosy lips and cheeks within his bending sickle's compass come. Love alters not with his brief hours and weeks, but bears it out even to the edge of doom. If this be error, and upon me prov'd, I never writ, nor no man ever loved.

Of Lust

→»×«←

IF THE balance of our lives had not one scale of reason to poise another of sensuality, the blood and baseness of our natures would conduct us to most prepost'rous conclusions; but we have reason to cool our raging motions, our carnal stings, our unbitted lusts, whereof I take this that you call love to be a sect or scion. . . . It is merely a lust of the blood and a permission of the will.

Th' expense of spirit in a waste of shame is lust in action; and till action, lust is perjur'd, murd'rous, bloody, full of blame, savage, extreme, rude, cruel, not to trust; enjoy'd no sooner but despised straight; past reason hunted; and no sooner had, past reason hated, as a swallowed bait on purpose laid to make the taker mad: mad in pursuit, and in possession so; had, having and in quest to have, extreme; a bliss in proof—and prov'd, a very woe; before, a joy propos'd; behind, a dream. All this the world well knows; yet none knows well to shun the heaven that leads men to this hell.

You cannot call it love; for at your age the hey-day in the blood is tame, it's humble, waits upon the judgment; and what judgment would step from this to this? Sense, sure, you have, else could you not have motion; but sure, that sense is apoplex'd; for madness would not err, nor sense to ecstasy was ne'er so thrall'd but it reserved some quantity of choice, to serve in such a difference. . . . Virtue as it never will be moved, though lewdness court it in a shape of heaven, so lust, though to a radiant angel link'd, will sate itself in a celestial bed and prey on garbage. Rebellious hell, if thou canst mutiny in a matron's bones, to flaming youth let virtue be as wax, and melt in her own fire. Proclaim no shame when the compulsive ardour gives the charge, since frost itself as actively doth burn, and reason panders will.

Call it not love, for Love to heaven is fled since sweating Lust on earth usurp'd his name; under whose simple semblance he hath fed upon fresh beauty, blotting it with blame; which the hot tyrant stains and soon bereaves, as caterpillars do the tender leaves. Love comforteth like sunshine after rain, but Lust's effect is tempest after sun; Love's gentle spring doth always fresh remain; Lust's winter comes ere summer half be done. Love surfeits not, Lust like a glutton dies; Love is all truth, Lust full of forged lies.

Marriage and Single Life

-»»««-

TELL me why thou wilt marry? My poor body requires it. I am driven on by the flesh; and he must needs go that the devil drives. I' th' blaze of youth, when oil and fire, too strong for reason's force, o'erbears it and burns on. We must be married, or we must live in bawdry. Will you be married? As the ox has his bow, the horse his curb, and the falcon her bells, so man hath his desires; and as pigeons bill, so wedlock would be nibbling.

Get you to church, and have a good priest that can tell you what marriage is. By marriage all little jealousies, which seem great, and all great fears, which import their dangers, would then be nothing.

Marriage is a matter of more worth than to be dealt in by attorneyship . . . for what is wedlock forced but a hell, an age of discord and continual strife? Whereas the contrary bringeth bliss and is a pattern of celestial peace. O curse of marriage, that we can call these delicate creatures ours, and not their appetites! I had rather be a toad and live upon the vapour of a dungeon than keep a corner in the thing I love for others' uses. Yet, 'tis the plague of great ones . . . 'tis destiny unshunnable, like death.

I will rather trust a Fleming with my butter . . . the

Welshman with my cheese, an Irishman with my aqua-
vitae bottle, or a thief to walk my ambling gelding, than
my wife with herself. Then she plots, then she rumi-
nates, then she devises; and what they think in their
hearts that may effect, they will break their hearts but
they will effect. The fittest time to corrupt a man's wife
is when she's fall'n out with her husband.

As horns are odious, they are necessary. . . . Many a
man has good horns and knows no end of them. Well,
that is the dowry of his wife; 'tis none of his own getting. Horns? Even so. . . . The noblest deer hath them
as huge as the rascal. Horns which such as you are fain
to be beholding to your wives for. What shall he have
that kill'd the deer? His leather skin and horns to wear.
Then sing him home. Take thou no scorn to wear the
horn; it was a crest ere thou wast born: thy father wore
it, and thy father bore it. The horn, the horn, the lusty
horn, is not a thing to laugh to scorn. He may sleep in
security; for he hath the horn of abundance, and the
lightness of his wife shines through it. Get thee a wife,
get thee a wife! There is no staff more reverend than
one tipp'd with horn. Should all despair that have re-
volted wives, the tenth of mankind would hang themselves. There have been (or I am much deceiv'd)
cuckolds ere now; and many a man there is (even at
this present, now) holds his wife by th' arm that little
thinks she has been sluic'd in 's absence and his pond
fish'd by his next neighbour—by Sir Smile, his neighbour. Nay, there's comfort in it. He that ears my land
spares my team and gives me leave to inn the crop. If I
be his cuckold, he's my drudge. . . . If men could be
[17]

contented to be what they are, there would be no fear in marriage.

A young man married is a man that's marr'd. She's not well married that lives married long, but she's best married that dies married young. If thou wilt needs marry, marry a fool; for wise men know well enough what monsters you make of them. Hasty marriage seldom proveth well. I know a wench married in an afternoon, as she went to the garden for parsley to stuff a rabbit. I have railed so long against marriage. In brief, since I do purpose to marry, I will think nothing to any purpose that the world can say against it.

But let still the woman take an elder than herself! so wears she to him, for, . . . however we do praise ourselves, our fancies are more giddy and unfirm, more longing, wavering, sooner lost and worn, than women's are. Earthlier happy is the rose distill'd than that which, withering on the virgin thorn, grows, lives, and dies in single blessedness.

Wives may be merry and yet honest too. I take today a wife whose beauty did astonish the survey of richest eyes; whose words all ears took captive; whose dear perfection hearts that scorn'd to serve humbly call'd mistress. That man i' th' world who shall report he has a better wife, let him in naught be trusted for speaking false in that: thou art, alone,—if thy rare qualities, sweet gentleness, thy meekness saint-like, wife-like government, obeying in commanding, and thy parts sovereign and pious else, could speak thee out,—the queen of earthly queens. Ye gods, render me worthy of this noble wife.

Of Ambition

-->>><<<-

I HOLD ambition of so airy and light a quality that it is but a shadow's shadow, a circle in the water, which never ceaseth to enlarge itself till by broad spreading it disperse to naught. Dreams indeed are ambition; for the very substance of the ambitious is merely the shadow of a dream. Ambition, the soldier's virtue, rather makes choice of loss than gain which darkens him, seeking the bubble reputation even in the cannon's mouth, makes mouths at the invisible event, exposing what is mortal and unsure to all that fortune, death, and danger dare, even for an eggshell.

Man and birds are fain of climbing high. Lowliness is young ambition's ladder, whereto the climber-upward turns his face; but when he once attains the upmost round, he then unto the ladder turns his back, looks in the clouds, scorning the base degrees by which he did ascend. And out of question, so it is sometimes: glory grows guilty of detested crimes when for fame's sake, for praise . . . we bend to that the workings of the heart. Th' abuse of greatness is when it disjoins remorse from power. Virtue is chok'd with foul ambition.

O! the fierce wretchedness that glory brings us! Vaulting ambition which o'erleaps itself and falls on th' other, thriftless ambition that wilt ravin up thine own live's means, which swell'd so much that it did almost stretch the sides o' th' world. Fling away ambition! By that sin fell the angels. How can man then (the image of his maker) hope to win by it? Vain pomp and glory of this world. . . . How wretched is that poor man that hangs on princes' favors! There is betwixt that smile we would aspire to, that sweet aspect of princes, and their ruin more pangs and fears than wars or women have: and when he falls, he falls like Lucifer, never to hope again. Better to be lowly born, and range with humble livers in content, than to be perk'd up in a glist'ring grief and wear a golden sorrow.

Fortune

-»>«<-

FORTUNE is painted blind, with a muffler afore her
eyes, to signify . . . that Fortune is blind; and she is
painted also with a wheel, to signify . . . which is the
moral of it, that she is turning and inconstant, and
mutability, and variation; and her foot, look you, is
fixed upon a spherical stone, which rolls, and rolls, and
rolls. In good truth, the poet makes a most excellent
description of it. Fortune is an excellent moral.

I have upon a high and pleasant hill feign'd Fortune
to be thron'd. The base o' th' mount is rank'd with all
deserts, all kinds of natures that labour on the bosom
of this sphere to propagate their states. Amongst them
all whose eyes are on this sovereign lady fix'd one do I
personate . . . whom Fortune with her ivory hand wafts
to her, whose present grace to present slaves and servants
translates his rivals. . . . This throne, this Fortune, and
this hill, methinks, with one man beckon'd from the
rest below, bowing his head against the steepy mount
to climb his happiness, would be well express'd in our
condition. . . . All those which were his fellows but of
late (some better than his value) on the moment follow
his strides, his lobbies fill with tendance, rain sacrificial
whisperings in his ear, make sacred even his stirrup, and
through him drink the free air. . . . When Fortune in her

[21]

shift and change of mood spurns down her late beloved, all his dependants, which labour'd after him to the mountain's top even on their knees and hands, let him slip down, not one accompanying his declining foot. 'Tis common. A thousand moral paintings I can show that shall demonstrate these quick blows of Fortune's more pregnantly than words.

Let us sit and mock the good housewife Fortune from her wheel, that her gifts may henceforth be bestowed equally. I would we could do so; for her benefits are mightily misplaced, and the bountiful blind woman doth most mistake in her gifts to women. . . . Those that she makes honest she makes very ill-favoredly. . . . When Nature hath made a fair creature, may she not by Fortune fall into the fire? Will Fortune never come with both hands full, but write her fair words still in foulest letters? She either gives a stomach, and no food (such are the poor in health) or else a feast, and takes away the stomach. O Fortune, Fortune, all men call thee fickle. Out, out, thou strumpet Fortune! All you gods, in general synod take away her power; break all the spokes and fellies from her wheel, and bowl the round nave down the hill of heaven.

Wisdom and fortune combatting together, if that the former dare but what it can, no chance may shake it. Fortune knows we scorn her most when most she offers blows. Fortune's blows when most struck home . . . craves a noble cunning.

Fortune brings in some boats that are not steer'd. Our indiscretion sometimes serves us well . . . and that

should teach us there's a divinity that shapes our ends,
rough-hew them how we will. I know not what counts
harsh fortune casts upon my face; but in my bosom
shall she never come to make my heart her vassal.

Of Sleep

->>><<<-

THY best of rest is sleep; sleep, that sometimes shuts up sorrow's eye, the golden dew of sleep, the innocent sleep, sleep that knits up the ravell'd sleave of care, the death of each day's life, sore labour's bath, balm of hurt minds, great nature's second course, chief nourisher in life's feast. These should be hours for necessities, not for delights; times to repair our nature with comforting repose.

Weary with toil, I haste me to my bed, the dear repose for limbs with travel tired; but then begins a journey in my head to work my mind when body's work's expired. . . . And keep my drooping eyelids open wide, looking on darkness which the blind do see. O sleep, O gentle sleep! Nature's soft nurse, how have I frighted thee, that thou no more wilt weigh my eyelids down and steep my senses in forgetfulness? Why rather, sleep, liest thou in smoky cribs, upon uneasy pallets stretching thee, and hush'd with buzzing night-flies to thy slumber, than in the perfum'd chambers of the great, under the canopies of costly state, and lull'd with sound of sweetest melody? O thou dull god, why liest thou with the vile in loathsome beds, and leav'st the kingly couch a watch case or a common 'larum-bell? Wilt thou upon the high and giddy mast seal up the shipboy's eyes, and rock his brains in cradle of the rude imperious surge, and in the visitation of the winds, who take the ruffian billows by the top, curling their monstrous heads, and hanging them with deaf'ning clamour in the slippery clouds, that with the hurly death itself awakes? Canst thou, O partial sleep, give thy repose to the wet seaboy in an hour so rude, and in the calmest and most stillest night, with all appliances and means to boot, deny it to a king? Then, happy low, lie down! 'Tis not the balm, the sceptre, and the ball, the sword, the mace, the crown imperial, the intertissued robe of gold and pearl, the farced title running fore the king, the throne he sits on, nor the tide of pomp that beats upon the high shore of this world—No, not all these, thrice-gorgeous ceremony, not all these, laid in bed majestical, can sleep so soundly as the wretched slave, who, with a body fill'd and vacant mind, gets him to rest, cramm'd with distressful bread; never sees horrid night, the child of hell; but like a lackey, from the rise to set, sweats in the eye of Phoebus, and all night sleeps in Elysium; next day after dawn, doth rise and help Hyperion to his horse; and follows so the ever-running year with profitable labour to his grave; and but for ceremony, such a wretch, winding up days with toil and nights with sleep, had the forehand and vantage of a king.

Of Friendship

>>><<<

I count myself in nothing else so happy as in a soul rememb'ring my good friends; and, as my fortune ripens with thy love, it shall be still thy true love's recompense.

What need we have any friends if we should ne'er have need of 'em? They were the most needless creatures living, should we ne'er have use for 'em; and would most resemble sweet instruments hung up in cases, that keep their sounds to themselves. Why, I have often wish'd myself poorer, that I might come nearer to you. We are born to do benefits; and what better or properer can we call our own than the riches of our friends? Thou dost conspire against thy friend, . . . if thou but think'st him wrong'd, and mak'st his ear a stranger to thy thoughts.

The amity that wisdom knits not, folly may easily untie. Friends now fast sworn, whose double bosom seems to wear one heart, whose hours, whose bed, whose meal and exercise are still together, who twin (as 'twere) in love unseparable, shall within this hour, on a dissension of a doit, break out to bitterest enmity. So fellest foes, whose passions and whose plots have broke their sleep to take the one the other, by some chance, some trick not worth an egg, shall grow dear friends and interjoin their issues. The great man down, you mark his favourite flies, the poor advanc'd makes friends of enemies; and hitherto doth love on fortune tend, for who not needs shall never lack a friend, and who in want a hollow friend doth try, directly seasons him his enemy.

Those friends thou hast, and their adoption tried, grapple them unto thy soul with hoops of steel; but do not dull thy palm with entertainment of each new-hatch'd, unfledg'd comrade. Hollow men, like horses hot at hand, make gallant show and promise of their mettle; but when they should endure the bloody spur, they fall their crest, and like deceitful jades sink in the trial. Where you are liberal of your loves and counsels be sure you be not loose; for those you make friends and give your hearts to, when they once perceive the least rub in your fortunes, fall away like water from ye, never found again but where they mean to sink ye.

He that wants money, means, and content is without three good friends.

Drinking—Against

O THOU invisible spirit of wine, if thou hast no name to be known by, let us call thee devil! God, that men should put an enemy in their mouths to steal away their brains! That we should with joy, pleasance, revel, and applause transform ourselves into beasts! Every inordinate cup is unblest, and the ingredience is a devil. It's monstrous labour when I wash my brain and it grows fouler. Drunk? and speak parrot? and squabble? swagger? swear? and discourse fustian with one's own shadow? Ingrateful man with liquorish draughts and morsels unctious greases his pure mind, that from it all consideration slips.

I learn'd it in England, where indeed they are most potent in potting. Your Dane, your German, and your swag-bellied Hollander . . . are nothing to your English. . . . Why, he drinks you with facility your Dane dead drunk; he sweats not to overthrow your Almain; he gives your Hollander a vomit ere the next pottle can be fill'd. Though I am native here and to the manner born, it is a custom more honour'd in the breach than the observance. This heavy-headed revel east and west makes us traduc'd . . . of other nations; they clip us drunkards and with swinish phrase soil our addition; and indeed it takes from our achievements, though perform'd at height, the pith and marrow of our attribute.

Drinking—For

-»»-«e-

COME, come, good wine is a good familiar creature if it be well us'd. Dost thou think, because thou art virtuous, there shall be no more cakes and ale?

There's never none of these demure boys come to any proof; for thin drink doth so over-cool their blood, and making many fish-meals, that they fall into a kind of male greensickness; and then, when they marry, they get wenches. They are generally fools and cowards— which some of us should be too, but for inflammation. A good sherris sack hath a twofold operation in it. It ascends me into the brain; dries me there all the foolish and dull and crudy vapours which environ it; makes it apprehensive, quick, forgetive, full of nimble, fiery, and delectable shapes; which delivered o'er to the voice, the tongue, which is the birth, becomes excellent wit. The second property of your excellent sherris is the warming of the blood; which before (cold and settled) left the liver white and pale, which is the badge of pusillanimity and cowardice; but the sherris warms it and makes it course from the inwards to the parts extremes. It illumineth the face, which, as a beacon, gives warning to all the rest of this little kingdom, man, to arm; and then the vital commoners and inland petty spirits muster me all to their captain, the heart; who, great and puff'd up with this retinue, doth any deed of courage. And this valour comes of sherris: so that skill in the weapon is nothing without sack, for that sets it awork; and learning a mere hoard of gold kept by a devil, till sack commences it and sets it in act and use. . . . If I had a thousand sons, the first humane principle I would teach them should be to forswear thin potations and to addict themselves to sack.

Of Ignorance and Learning

→»-«←

THERE is no darkness but ignorance, gross and misera-
ble ignorance. Thou monster, the common curse of
mankind, how deformed dost thou look. Dull, unfeel-
ing, barren ignorance, thou praisest the worst best.
Ignorant as dirt, an idiot holds his bauble for a god.
We, ignorant of ourselves, beg often our own harms.
What a thrice-double ass was I to take this drunkard for
a god and worship this dull fool!

Ignorance is the curse of God, knowledge the wing
wherewith we fly to heaven. O this learning, what a
thing it is! And though I have for barbarism spoke
more than for that angel knowledge, I held it ever
virtue and cunning were endowments greater than no-
bleness and riches. Careless heirs may the two latter
darken and expend; but immortality attends the former, making a man a god. Fitter is my study and my
books than wanton dalliance.

What is the end of study? Let me know. Why, that
to know which else we should not know. Things hid
and barr'd . . . from common sense . . . that is study's
godlike recompense. If study's gain be thus, study is like
the heaven's glorious sun, that will not be deep search'd
with saucy looks.

Universal plodding prisons up the nimble spirits in

the arteries. Small have continual plodders ever won save base authority from other's books. So study evermore is overshot. While it doth study to have what it would, it doth forget to do the thing it should; and when it hath the thing it hunteth most, 'tis won as towns with fire—so won, so lost. All delights are vain, but that most vain which, with pain purchas'd, doth inherit pain: as, painfully to pore upon a book to seek the light of truth while truth the while doth falsely blind the eyesight of his look. Light, seeking light, doth light of light beguile. So, ere you find where light in darkness lies, your light grows dark by losing of your eyes. These earthly godfathers of heaven's lights that give a name to every fixed star have no more profit of their shining nights than those that walk and wot not what they are.

None are so surely caught, when they are catch'd, as wit turn'd fool. Folly, in wisdom hatch'd, hath wisdom's warrant, and the help of school, and wit's own grace to grace a learned fool. O Knowledge ill-inhabited, worse than Jove in a thatch'd house!

In brief . . . study what you most affect. Our bodies are our gardens, to the which our wills are gardeners. The even mead, that erst brought sweetly forth the freckled cowslip, burnet, and green clover, wanting the scythe, all uncorrected, rank, conceives by idleness and nothing teems but hateful docks, rough thistles, kecksies, burrs, losing both beauty and utility. And as our vineyards, fallows, meads, and hedges, defective in their natures, grow to wildness, even so our houses and ourselves and children have lost, or do not learn for want of time, the sciences that should become our country.

[32]

Of Philosophy

→»·«←

WE HAVE our philosophical persons, to make modern
and familiar, things supernatural and causeless. Hence
it is that we make trifles of terrors, ensconcing ourselves into seeming knowledge.

Hang up philosophy! Unless philosophy can make a
Juliet, displant a town, reverse a prince's doom, it helps
not, it prevails not. Who can hold a fire in his hand by
thinking on the frosty Caucasus? Or cloy the hungry
edge of appetite by bare imagination of a feast? Or wal-
low naked in December snow by thinking on fantastic
summer's heat? O, no! the apprehension of the good gives
but the greater feeling to the worse. For there was never
yet philosopher that could endure the toothache pa-
tiently, however they have writ the style of gods and
made a push at chance and sufferance. A wretched soul
bruis'd with adversity we bid be quiet when we hear
it cry; but were we burd'ned with like weight of pain,
as much, or more, we should ourselves complain.
Brother, men can counsel and speak comfort to that
grief which they themselves not feel; but, tasting it,
their counsel turns to passion, which before would
give preceptial medicine to rage, fetter strong madness
in a silken thread, charm ache with air and agony with
words. No, no; 'tis all men's office to speak patience to
those that wring under the load of sorrow, but no

[33]

man's virtue nor sufficiency to be so moral when he shall endure the like himself. It is a good divine that follows his own instructions. I can easier teach twenty what were good to be done than to be one of the twenty to follow mine own teaching.

These deeds must not be thought after these ways, sicklied o'er with the pale cast of thought. You do unbend your noble strength to think so brainsickly of things. Of your philosophy you make no use if you give place to accidental evils. To be generous, guiltless, and of free disposition, is to take those things for birdbolts that you deem cannon bullets. There is nothing either good or bad but thinking makes it so. All places that the eye of heaven visits are to a wise man ports and happy havens.

Of the Virtue of Laughter

LET us say you are sad, because you are not merry; and 'twere as easy for you to laugh and leap, and say you are merry because you are not sad. Now, by two-headed Janus, nature hath fram'd strange fellows in her time: some that will evermore peep through their eyes, and laugh like parrots at a bag-piper; and others of such vinegar aspect that they'll not show their teeth in way of smile, though Nestor swear the jest be laughable. . . .

You have too much respect upon the world; they lose it that do buy it with much care. . . . Let me play the fool. With mirth and laughter let old wrinkles come, and let my liver rather heat with wine than my heart cool with mortifying groans. A merry heart lives long. A merry heart goes all the day, your sad tires in a mile. Why should a man whose blood is warm within, sit like his grandsire cut in alabaster? sleep when he wakes? and creep into the jaundice by being peevish? I tell thee what, . . . There are a sort of men whose visages do cream and mantle like a standing pond, and do a wilful stillness entertain, with purpose to be dress'd in an opinion of wisdom, gravity, profound conceit; as who should say, 'I am Sir Oracle, and when I ope my lips let no dog bark. . . . ' I do know of these, that therefore only are reputed wise for saying nothing; when, I am very sure, if they should speak, would almost damn those ears which, hearing them, would call their brothers fools. Seeing too much sadness has congeal'd your blood and melancholy is the nurse of frenzy, therefore . . . frame your mind to mirth and merriment, which bars a thousand harms and lengthens life.

Of Mental Pain

-->>><<<-

BETTER be with the dead . . . than on the torture of the mind to lie in restless ecstasy. Better I were distract. So should my thoughts be sever'd from my griefs, and woes by wrong imaginations lose the knowledge of themselves. I am bound upon a wheel of fire, that mine own tears do scald like molten lead. Canst thou . . . minister to a mind diseas'd, pluck from the memory a rooted sorrow, raze out the written troubles of the brain, and with some sweet oblivious antidote cleanse the stuff'd bosom of that perilous stuff which weighs upon the heart? Not poppy nor mandragora, nor all the drowsy syrups of the world, shall ever medicine thee to that sweet sleep thou ow'dst yesterday.

Some griefs are med'cinable. We are not ourselves when nature, being oppress'd, commands the mind to suffer with the body. Each substance of a grief hath twenty shadows. Grief would have tears. Give sorrow words. The grief that does not speak whispers the o'er-fraught heart and bids it break. Sorrow concealed, like an oven stopp'd, doth burn the heart to cinders where it is. Deep sounds make lesser noise than shallow fords, and sorrow ebbs, being blown with wind of words. Sorrow breaks seasons and reposing hours, makes the night

[37]

morning and the noontide night. Grief dallied with
nor law nor limit knows.

When sorrows come, they come not single spies, but
in battalions. One sorrow never comes but brings an
heir that may succeed as his inheritor. For sorrow, like
a heavy hanging bell, once set on ringing, with his own
weight goes.

Oft have I heard that grief softens the mind and
makes it fearful and degenerate. Moderate lamentation
is the right of the dead; excessive grief the enemy to
the living. If the living be enemy to the grief, the excess makes it soon mortal. But to persever in obstinate
condolement is a course of impious stubbornness. 'Tis
unmanly grief; it shows a will most incorrect to heaven,
a heart unfortified, a mind impatient, an understanding
simple and unschool'd. This is the poison of deep grief.

What's gone and what's past help should be past
grief. Things without all remedy should be without
regard. What's done is done. He robs himself that
spends a bootless grief. Gnarling sorrow hath less power
to bite the man that mocks at it and sets it light.

In poison there is physic, and these news, having been
well, that would have made me sick, being sick, have
in some measure made me well; and as the wretch
whose fever-weak'ned joints, like strengthless hinges,
buckle under life, impatient of his fit, breaks like a
fire out of his keeper's arms, even so my limbs, weak-
ened with grief, being now enrag'd with grief are thrice
themselves. To be worst, the lowest and most dejected
thing of fortune, stands still in esperance, lives not in
fear. The lamentable change is from the best; the worst
returns to laughter.

[38]

Of the Force of the Imagination

→≫≪←

I TALK of dreams; which are the children of an idle brain, begot of nothing but vain fantasy; which is as thin of substance as the air, and more inconstant than the wind, who woos even now the frozen bosom of the north and, being anger'd, puffs away from thence, turning his face to the dew-dropping south. You laugh when boys or women tell their dreams. The best in this kind are but shadows; and the worst are no worse, if imagination amend them.

Such tricks hath strong imagination that, if it would but apprehend some joy, it comprehends some bringer of that joy; or in the night, imagining some fear, how easy is a bush suppos'd a bear! Lovers and madmen have such seething brains, such shaping fantasies, that apprehend more than cool reason ever comprehends. The lunatic, the lover, and the poet are of imagination all compact. One sees more devils than vast hell can hold: that is the madman. The lover, all as frantic, sees Helen's beauty in a brow of Egypt. There may be in the cup a spider steep'd, and one may drink, depart, and yet partake no venom, for his knowledge is not infected; but if one present th' abhorr'd ingredient to his eye, make known how he hath drunk, he cracks his gorge, his sides, with violent hefts. The sense of death is most in apprehension, and the poor beetle that we tread upon, in corporal sufferance finds a pang as great as when a giant dies.

Fools . . . in th' imagination set the goodly objects which abroad they find of lands and mansions, theirs in thought assign'd, and labouring in more pleasures to bestow them than the true gouty landlord which doth owe them.

Present fears are less than horrible imaginings. I yield to that suggestion whose horrid image doth unfix my hair and make my seated heart knock at my ribs against the use of nature. . . . My thought, . . . but fantastical, shakes so my single state of man that function is smother'd in surmise and nothing is but what is not. I could be bounded in a nutshell and count myself a king of infinite space, were it not that I have bad dreams.

On Life

->>> <<<-

LIFE is a shuttle. The web of our life is of a mingled yarn, good and ill together. The single and peculiar life is bound with all the strength and armour of the mind to keep itself from noyance with ... incident throes that nature's fragile vessel doth sustain in life's uncertain voyage.

How brief the life of man runs his erring pilgrimage. A man's life no more than to say "one."

It is silliness to live when to live is torment; that life is better life, past fearing death, than that which lives to fear.

My life I never held but as a pawn; there's nothing serious in mortality; all is but toys; renown and grace is dead; the wine of life is drawn, and the mere lees is left this vault to brag of: as flies to wanton boys, are we to th' gods. They kill us for their sport. When we are born, we cry that we are come to this great stage of fools; we came crying hither; thou know'st, the first time that we smell the air we waul and cry; men must endure their going hence, even as their coming hither; ripeness is all. 'Tis but an hour ago since it was nine, and after an hour more 'twill be eleven; and so, from hour to hour, we ripe, and then from hour to hour we rot and rot; and thereby hangs a tale.

[41]

This is the state of man: to-day he puts forth the tender leaves of hope; to-morrow blossoms and bears his blushing honours thick upon him; the third day comes a frost, a killing frost, and when he thinks, good easy man, full surely his greatness is a-ripening, nips his root, and then he falls. Life's but a walking shadow, a poor player, that struts and frets his hour upon the stage and then is heard no more. It is a tale told by an idiot, full of sound and fury, signifying nothing.

The weariest and most loathed worldly life that age, ache, penury, and imprisonment can lay on nature is a paradise to what we fear of death. Let me live in a dungeon, i' th' stocks, or anywhere, so I may live. Simply the thing I am shall make me live.

Adversity

->>><<<-

To WILFUL men the injuries that they themselves procure must be their schoolmasters.

The art of our necessities is strange, that can make vile things precious. Nothing almost sees miracles but misery. You were us'd to say extremity was the trier of spirits; that common chances common men could bear; that when the sea was calm, all boats alike show'd mastership in floating. The sea being smooth, how many shallow bauble boats dare sail upon her patient breast, making their way with those of nobler bulk! But let the ruffian Boreas once enrage the gentle Thetis, and anon behold the strong-ribb'd bark through liquid mountains cut. . . . Where's then the saucy boat whose weak untimber'd sides but even now corrivall'd greatness? Either to harbor fled or made a toast for Neptune. In the reproof of chance lies the true proof of men.

I'll give thee armour . . . adversity's sweet milk, philosophy. What thy soul holds dear, imagine it to lie that way thou goest, not whence thou com'st. Suppose the singing birds musicians, the grass whereon thou tread'st the presence strow'd, the flowers fair ladies, and thy steps no more than a delightful measure or a dance.

They are as sick that surfeit with too much as they that starve with nothing. It is no mean happiness, therefore, to be seated in the mean. Superfluity comes sooner by white hairs, but competency lives longer. Our basest beggars are in the poorest thing superfluous. Allow not nature more than nature needs, man's life is cheap as beast's. . . . If only to go warm were gorgeous, why, nature needs not what thou gorgeous wear'st, which scarcely keeps thee warm.

Checks and disasters grow in the veins of actions highest rear'd, as knots, by the conflux of meeting sap, infects the sound pine, and diverts his grain tortive and errant from his course of growth.

There is some soul of goodness in things evil. . . . Our bad neighbor makes us early stirrers, which is both healthful, and good husbandry. Besides, they are our outward consciences, and preachers to us all, admonishing that we should dress us fairly for our end. Thus may we gather honey from the weed and make a moral of the devil himself. 'Tis good for men to love their present pains upon example: so the spirit is eas'd; and when the mind is quick'ned, out of doubt the organs, though defunct and dead before, break up their drowsy grave and newly move with casted slough and fresh legerity.

The worst is not so long as we can say 'This is the worst.'

Of Death

-»»«‹-

REASON thus with life: if I do lose thee, I do lose a
thing that none but fools would keep. A breath thou
art, servile to all the skyey influences that do this habitation where thou keep'st hourly afflict. Merely thou
art death's fool; for him thou labour'st by thy flight to
shun, and yet runn'st toward him still. Thou art not
noble; for all th' accommodations that thou bear'st are
nurs'd by baseness. Thou'rt by no means valiant; for
thou dost fear the soft and tender fork of a poor worm.
Thy best of rest is sleep, and that thou oft provok'st;
yet grossly fear'st thy death, which is no more. Thou
art not thyself; for thou exist'st on many a thousand
grains that issue out of dust. Happy thou art not; for
what thou hast not, still thou striv'st to get, and what
thou hast, forget'st. Thou art not certain; for thy complexion shifts to strange effects, after the moon. If thou
art rich, thou'rt poor; for, like an ass whose back with
ingots bows, thou bear'st thy heavy riches but a journey, and death unloads thee. Friend hast thou none;
for thine own bowels which do call thee sire, the mere
effusion of thy proper loins, do curse the gout, serpigo,
and the rheum for ending thee no sooner. Thou hast
nor youth nor age, but as it were an after-dinner's sleep,
dreaming on both; for all thy blessed youth becomes as

[45]

aged, and doth beg the alms of palsied eld; and when thou art old and rich, thou hast neither heat, affection, limb, nor beauty to make thy riches pleasant. What's yet in this that bears the name of life?

To sue to live, I find I seek to die; and seeking death, find life. Let it come on . . . if it be now, 'tis not to come; if it be not to come, it will be now; if it be not now, yet it will come: the readiness is all. Since no man knows aught of what he leaves, what is't to leave it betimes? Cowards die many times before their deaths; the valiant never taste of death but once. Of all the wonders that I yet have heard, it seems to me most strange that men should fear, seeing that death, a necessary end, will come when it will come. . . . Within the hollow crown that rounds the mortal temples of a king keeps Death his court; and there the antic sits, scoffing his state and grinning at his pomp; allowing him a breath, a little scene, to monarchize, be fear'd, and kill with looks; infusing him with self and vain conceit, as if this flesh which walls about our life were brass impregnable; and humour'd thus, comes at the last, and with a little pin bores through his castle wall, and farewell king!

Fear no more the heat o' th' sun nor the furious winter's rages; thou thy worldly task hast done, home art gone, and ta'en thy wages. Golden lads and girls all must, as chimney-sweepers, come to dust. Fear no more the frown o' th' great; thou art past the tyrant's stroke. Care no more to clothe and eat; to thee the reed is as the oak. The sceptre, learning, physic, must all follow this and come to dust.

Suicide, Against and For

→»«←

AGAINST self-slaughter, there is a prohibition so divine that cravens my weak hand. O, our lives' sweetness! that we the pain of death would hourly die rather than die at once. I know not how, but I do find it cowardly and vile, for fear of what might fall, so to prevent the time of life—arming myself with patience to stay the providence of some high powers that govern us here below.

O . . . that the Everlasting had not fix'd his canon 'gainst self-slaughter! Is wretchedness deprived that benefit to end itself by death? 'Twas yet some comfort when misery could beguile the tyrant's rage and frustrate his proud will. Therein, ye gods, you make the weak most strong; therein you tyrants do defeat. Nor stony tower, nor walls of beaten brass, nor airless dungeon, nor strong links of iron can be retentive to the strength of spirit; but life being weary of these worldly bars never lacks power to dismiss itself. . . . That part of tyranny that I do bear, I can shake off at pleasure. Our dungy earth breeds beast as man. And it is great to do that deed that ends all other deeds, which shackles accidents and bolts up change, which sleeps and never palates more the dung, the beggar's nurse and Caesar's.

[47]

Of Riches

→»«←

How quickly nature falls into revolt when gold becomes her object! For this the foolish over-careful
fathers have broke their sleep with thoughts, their
brains with care, their bones with industry; for this
they have engrossed and pil'd up the cank'red heaps of
strange-achieved gold; for this they have been thought-
ful to invest their sons with arts and martial exercises:
when, like the bee, tolling from every flower the virtuous sweets, our thighs pack'd with wax, our mouths
with honey, we bring it to the hive, and, like the bees,
are murd'red for our pains. This bitter taste yields his
engrossments to the ending father.

'Tis gold which buys admittance; oft it doth—yea,
and makes Diana's rangers false themselves, yield up
their deer to th' stand o' th' stealer; and 'tis gold which
makes the true man kill'd and saves the thief; nay,
sometimes hangs both thief and true man. What can it
not do? 'Tis certain, greatness, once fall'n out with fortune, must fall out with men too. What the declin'd is
he shall as soon read in the eyes of others as feel in his
own fall; for men, like butterflies, show not their mealy
wings but to the summer; and not a man for being
simply man hath any honour, but honour for those
honours that are without him, as place, riches, and fa-

vour, prizes of accident as oft as merit; which when they fall, as being slippery standers, the love that lean'd on them as slippery too, doth one pluck down another, and together die in the fall.

Gold! Yellow, glittering, precious gold! . . . Thus much of this will make black white, foul fair, wrong right, base noble, old young, coward valiant. . . . Why, this will lug your priests and servants from your sides, pluck sick men's pillows from below their heads: this yellow slave will knit and break religions, bless th' accurs'd, make the hoar leprosy ador'd, place thieves and give them title, knee, and approbation with senators on the bench. This is it that makes the wappen'd widow wed again; she whom the spital-house and ulcerous sores would cast the gorge at, this embalms and spices to th' April day again. O thou sweet king-killer, and dear divorce 'twixt natural son and sire! thou bright defiler of Hymen's purest bed! thou valiant Mars! thou ever young, fresh, lov'd, and delicate wooer, whose blush doth thaw the consecrated snow that lies on Dian's lap! thou visible god, that sold'rest close impossibilities and mak'st them kiss! that speak'st with every tongue to every purpose!

On Ceremony

->>><<<-

WHAT infinite heart's-ease must kings neglect that private men enjoy! And what have kings that privates have not too, save ceremony, save general ceremony? And what art thou, thou idol Ceremony? What kind of god art thou, that suffer'st more of mortal griefs than do thy worshippers? What are thy rents? What are thy comings-in? O Ceremony, show me but thy worth! What is thy soul of adoration? Art thou aught else but place, degree, and form, creating awe and fear in other men? Wherein thou art less happy being fear'd than they in fearing. What drink'st thou oft, instead of homage sweet, but poison'd flattery? Ceremony was but devis'd at first to set a gloss on faint deeds, hollow welcomes, recanting goodness, sorry ere 'tis shown; but where there is true friendship, there needs none.

Be sick, great greatness, and bid thy ceremony give thee cure! Think'st thou the fiery fever will go out with titles blown from adulation? Will it give place to flexure and low bending? Canst thou, when thou command'st the beggar's knee, command the health of it? No, thou proud dream. . . .

Behold how pomp is followed! What need these feasts, pomps and vain glories? To be possess'd with double pomp, to guard a title that was rich before, to gild refined gold, . . . is wasteful and ridiculous excess. Vain pomp and glory of this world I hate ye; let the candied tongue lick absurd pomp, and crook the pregnant hinges of the knee where thrift may follow fawning. What is pomp, rule, reign, but earth and dust? O the fierce wretchedness that glory brings us! Who would not wish to be from wealth exempt, since riches point to misery and contempt? Who would be so mock'd with glory or to live but in a dream of friendship, to have his pomp, and all what state compounds, but only painted like his varnish'd friends?

Willing misery outlives incertain pomp, is crowned before. The one is filling still, never complete; the other, at high wish. Best state, contentless, hath a distracted and most wretched being, worse than the worst content. I am for the house with the narrow gate, which I take to be too little for pomp to enter. Some that humble themselves may; but the many will be too chill and tender. And they'll be for the flow'ry way that leads to the broad gate and the great fire, the primrose way to th' everlasting bonfire.

Of Mobs

→→→≪≪≪

WHAT would you have, you curs, that like nor peace nor war? The one affrights you, the other makes you proud. He that trusts to you, where he should find you lions, finds you hares; where foxes, geese. You are no surer, no, than is the coal of fire upon the ice or hailstone in the sun. Your virtue is to make him worthy whose offence subdues him, and curse that justice did it. Who deserves greatness deserves your hate; and your affections are a sick man's appetite, who desires most that which would increase his evil. He that depends upon your favours swims with fins of lead and hews down oaks with rushes. Hang ye! Trust ye? With every minute you do change a mind, and call him noble that was now your hate, him vile that was your garland. . . . They'll sit by th' fire, and presume to know what's done i' the Capitol, who's like to rise, who thrives, and who declines; side factions, and give out conjectural marriages; making parties strong, and feebling such as stand not in their liking below their cobbled shoes. It hath been taught us from the primal state, that he which is was wish'd until he were; and the ebb'd man, ne'er lov'd till ne'er worth love, comes dear'd by being lack'd. This common body, like to a vagabond flag upon the stream, goes to and back, lackeying the varying tide, to rot itself with motion.

An habitation giddy and unsure hath he that buildeth on the vulgar heart. O thou fond Many! with what loud applause didst thou beat heaven with blessing Bolingbroke, before he was what thou wouldst have him be! And being now trimm'd in thine own desires . . . thou art so full of him, that thou provok'st thyself to cast him up. So, so . . . didst thou disgorge thy glutton bosom of the royal Richard; and now thou wouldst eat thy dead vomit up, and howl'st to find it. What trust is in these times? Was ever feather so lightly blown to and fro as is this multitude?

On the Injustice of Society

O THAT estates, degrees, and offices were not deriv'd corruptly, and that clear honor were purchas'd by the merit of the wearer! How many then should cover that stand bare! How many be commanded that command! How much low peasantry would then be gleaned from the true seed of honour! and how much honour pick'd from the chaff and ruin of the times to be new varnish'd!

A man may see how the world goes with no eyes. Look with thine ears. See how yond justice rails upon yond simple thief. Hark in thine ear. Change places and, handy-dandy, which is the justice, which is the thief? Thou hast seen a farmer's dog bark at a beggar? . . . And the creature run from the cur? There thou mightst behold the great image of authority: a dog's obey'd in office. Thou rascal beadle, hold thy bloody hand! Why dost thou lash that whore? Strip thine own back. Thou hotly lusts to use her in that kind for which thou whip'st her. The usurer hangs the cozener. Through tatter'd clothes small vices do appear; robes and furr'd gowns hide all. Plate sin with gold, and the strong lance of justice hurtless breaks; arm it in rags, a pigmy's straw does pierce it. The jury, passing on the prisoner's life, may in the sworn twelve have a thief or two guiltier than him they try. . . . What knows the law that thieves do

[54]

pass on thieves? The blind mole casts copp'd hills towards heaven, to tell the earth is throng'd by man's
oppression, and the poor worm doth die for 't. Raise me
this beggar and deny't that lord: the senator shall bear
contempt hereditary, the beggar native honor. It is the
pasture lards the rother's sides, the want that makes him
lean.

Tir'd with all these, for restful death I cry: as, to behold desert a beggar born, and needy nothing trimm'd
in jollity, and purest faith unhappily forsworn, and
gilded honor shamefully misplac'd, and maiden virtue
rudely strumpeted, and right perfection wrongfully disgrac'd, and strength by limping sway disabled, and art
made tongue-tied by authority, and folly (doctor-like)
controlling skill, and simple truth miscall'd simplicity,
and captive good attending captain ill. Tir'd with all
these, from these would I be gone.

Retributive Justice

-»>)«<-

JUSTICE always whirls in equal measure. In the corrupted currents of the world offence's gilded hand may shove by justice, and oft 'tis seen the wicked prize itself buys out the law; but 'tis not so above. There is no shuffling; there sits a judge that no king can corrupt; there the action lies in his true nature, and we ourselves compell'd, even to the teeth and forehead of our faults, to give in evidence.

He that steeps his safety in true blood shall find but bloody safety and untrue. If th' assassination could trammel up the consequence . . . that but this blow might be the be-all and the end-all here, but here, upon this bank and shoal of time, we'ld jump the life to come. But in these cases we still have judgment here, that we but teach bloody instructions, which, being taught, return to plague th' inventor. This even-handed justice commends th' ingredience of our poison'd chalice to our own lips. The gods are just, and of our pleasant vices make instruments to plague us. He that of greatest works is finisher oft does them by the weakest minister. Foul deeds will rise, though all the earth o'erwhelm them, to men's eyes. For murther, though it have no tongue, will speak with most miraculous organ.

Know'st thou not that when the seaching eye of

heaven is hid behind the globe, that lights the lower world, then thieves and robbers range abroad unseen in murthers and in outrage boldly here; but when from under this terrestrial ball he fires the proud tops of the Eastern pines and darts his light through every guilty hole, then murthers, treasons, and detested sins, the cloak of night being pluck'd from off their backs, stand bare and naked, trembling at themselves? Tremble, thou wretch, that hast within thee undivulged crimes un-whipp'd of justice. Hide thee, thou bloody hand; thou perjur'd, and thou simular man of virtue that art inces-tuous. Caitiff, in pieces shake that under covert and con-venient seeming hast practis'd on man's life. . . . Beyond the infinite and boundless reach of mercy, if thou didst this deed of death, art thou damn'd. . . . Do but despair; and if thou want'st a cord, the smallest thread that ever spider twisted from her womb will serve to strangle thee; a rush will be a beam to hang thee on. Or wouldst thou drown thyself, put but a little water in a spoon, and it shall be as all the ocean, enough to stifle such a villain up. . . . Close pent-up guilts, rive your concealing con-tinents, and cry these dreadful summoners grace. If that the heavens do not their visible spirits send quickly down to tame these vile offences, it will come, humanity must perforce prey on itself, like monsters of the deep.

Of Responsibility for Crime

➜➤)(≪⮜

THESE late eclipses in the sun and moon portend no good to us. Though the wisdom of nature can reason it thus, yet nature finds itself scourg'd by the sequent effects. Love cools, friendship falls off, brothers divide. In cities, mutinies; in countries, discord; in palaces, treason; and the bond crack'd 'twixt son and father . . . unnaturalness between the child and the parent; death, dearth, dissolutions of ancient amities; divisions in state, menaces and maledictions against king and nobles; needless diffidences, banishment of friends, dissipation of cohorts, nuptial breaches. . . . We have seen the best of our time. Machinations, hollowness, treachery, and all ruinous disorders follow us disquietly to our graves.

This is the excellent foppery of the world, that, when we are sick in fortune, often the surfeit of our own behaviour, we make guilty of our disasters the sun, the moon, and the stars; as if we were villains on necessity; fools by heavenly compulsion; knaves, thieves, and treachers by spherical predominance; drunkards, liars, and adulterers by an enforc'd obedience of planetary influence; and all that we are evil in, by a divine thrusting on. An admirable evasion of whoremaster man, to lay his goatish disposition on the charge of a star! My father compounded with my mother under the Dragon's

[58]

Tail, and my nativity was under Ursa Major, so that it follows I am rough and lecherous. Fut! I should have been that I am, had the maidenliest star in the firmament twinkled on my bastardizing.

'Tis in ourselves that we are thus or thus. Our bodies are our gardens, to the which our wills are gardeners; so that if we will plant nettles or sow lettuce, set hyssop and weed up thyme, supply it with one gender of herbs or distract it with many—either to have it sterile with idleness or manured with industry—why, the power and corrigible authority of this lies in our wills. Our remedies oft in ourselves do lie, which we ascribe to heaven. The fated sky gives us free scope; only doth backward pull our slow designs when we ourselves are dull. . . . Impossible be strange attempts to those that weight their pains in sense, and do suppose what hath been cannot be. The fault . . . is not in our stars, but in ourselves, that we are underlings.

Of Honour

->>><<<-

Honours thrive when rather from our acts we them derive, than our foregoers. The mere word's a slave, debosh'd on every tomb, on every grave a lying trophy; and as oft is dumb where dust and damn'd oblivion is the tomb of honour'd bones indeed. From lowest place, when virtuous things proceed, the place is dignified by th' doer's deed. Where great additions swell's, and virtue none, it is a dropsied honour. Good alone is good without a name; vileness is so: the property by what it is should go, not by the title. 'Tis the mind that makes the body rich; and as the sun breaks through the darkest clouds, so honour peereth in the meanest habit. If you were born to honour, show it now; ... make the judgment good that thought you worthy of it. The time of life is short! To spend that shortness basely were too long, if life did ride upon a dial's point still ending at the arrival of an hour.

Can honour set to a leg? No. Or an arm? No. Or take away the grief of a wound? No. Honour hath no skill in surgery, then? No. What is honour? A word. What is in that word honour? Air. A trim reckoning! Who hath it? He that dies a Wednesday. Doth he feel it? No. Doth he hear it? No. 'Tis insensible then? Yea, to the dead. But

[60]

will it not live with the living? No. Why? Detraction will not suffer it.

The fewer men, the greater share of honour. Honour travels in a strait so narrow where one but goes abreast. Keep then the path, for emulation hath a thousand sons that one by one pursue. If you give way, or hedge aside from the direct forthright, like to an ent'red tide they all rush by and leave you hindmost; or, like a gallant horse fall'n in first rank, lie there for pavement to the abject rear, o'errun and trampled on. Then what they do in present, though less than yours in past, must o'ertop yours.

By heaven, methinks it were an easy leap to pluck bright honour from the pale-fac'd moon, or dive into the bottom of the deep, where fathomline could never touch the ground, and pluck up drowned honour by the locks. Set honour in one eye and death i' th' other, and I will look on both indifferently; for let the gods so speed me as I love the name of honour more than I fear death. If it be a sin to covet honour, I am the most offending soul alive. Mine honour is my life.... Take honour from me and my life is done.

On Beauty

>>><<<

THE ornament of beauty is suspect. Nature with a beauteous wall doth oft close in pollution. Look on beauty, and you shall see 'tis purchas'd by the weight, which therein works a miracle in nature, making them lightest which wear most of it. So are those crisped snaky golden locks which make such wanton gambols with the wind upon supposed fairness often known to be the dowry of a second head, the skull that bred them, in the sepulchre. The power of beauty will sooner transform honesty from what it is to a bawd than the force of honesty can translate beauty into his likeness.

Beauty is but a vain and doubtful good; a shining gloss that fadeth suddenly; a flower that dies when first it 'gins to bud; a brittle glass that's broken presently; a doubtful good, a gloss, a glass, a flower, lost, faded, broken, dead within an hour; . . . beauty too rich for use, for earth too dear, . . . blemish'd once, for ever lost. Since brass, nor stone, nor earth, nor boundless sea, but sad mortality o'ersways their power, how with this rage shall beauty hold a plea, whose action is no stronger than a flower? O, how shall summer's honey breath hold out against the wrackful siege of batt'ring days, when rocks impregnable are not so stout, nor gates of steel so strong, but Time decays? When forty winters shall besiege thy

[62]

brow and dig deep trenches in thy beauty's field, thy youth's proud livery, so gaz'd on now, will be a tatter'd weed of small worth held.

Beauty's crest becomes the heavens well. When would you . . . have found the ground of study's excellence without the beauty of a woman's face? From women's eyes this doctrine I derive. They sparkle still the right Promethean fire; they are the books, the arts, the academes, that show, contain, and nourish all the world. For where is any author in the world teaches such beauty as a woman's eye? . . . Other slow arts entirely keep the brain . . . but love, first learned in a lady's eyes, lives not alone immured in the brain, but with the motion of all elements courses as swift as thought in every power, and gives to every power a double power.

From fairest creatures we desire increase, that thereby beauty's rose might never die.

Of Music

→→→》《←←←

KNOW the cause why music was ordain'd! Was it not to refresh the mind of man after his studies or his usual pain?

Music oft hath such a charm to make bad good. Do but note a wild and wanton herd, or race of youthful and unhandled colts, fetching mad bounds, bellowing and neighing loud, which is the hot condition of their blood: if they but hear perchance a trumpet sound, or any air of music touch their ears, you shall perceive them make a mutual stand, their savage eyes turn'd to a modest gaze by the sweet power of music. Therefore the poet did feign that Orpheus drew trees, stones, and floods, for Orpheus' lute was strung with poet's sinews, whose golden touch could soften steel and stones, make tigers tame, and huge leviathans forsake unsounded deeps to dance on sands. Naught so stockish, hard, and full of rage but music for the time doth change his nature. The man that hath no music in himself, nor is not mov'd with concord of sweet sounds, is fit for treasons, stratagems, and spoils; the motions of his spirit are dull as night, and his affections dark as Erebus. Let no such man be trusted.

How sour sweet music is when time is broke and no proportion kept! Soft stillness and the night become the touches of sweet harmony. . . . Look how the floor of heaven is thick inlaid with patines of bright gold: there's not the smallest orb which thou behold'st but in his motion like an angel sings. . . . Such harmony is in immortal souls; but whilst this muddy vesture of decay doth grossly close it in, we cannot hear it.

So it is in the music of men's lives. The tongues of dying men enforce attention like deep harmony. . . . The setting sun, and music at the close, as the last taste of sweets, is sweetest last, writ in remembrance more than things long past.

Poetry

➤➤➤◄◄◄

I DO not know what poetical is. Is it honest in deed and word? These fellows of infinite tongue, that can rhyme themselves into ladies' favours, they do always reason themselves out again. The truest poetry is the most feigning, and lovers are given to poetry; and what they swear in poetry may be said, as lovers, they do feign. When the blood burns, how prodigal the soul lends the tongue vows. At lovers' perjuries, they say Jove laughs. What! A speaker is but a prater; a rhyme is but a ballad. I had rather be a kitten and cry mew than one of these same metre ballad-mongers. I had rather hear a brazen canstick turn'd or a dry wheel grate on the axletree, and that would set my teeth nothing on edge, nothing so much as mincing poetry. 'Tis like the forc'd gait of a shuffling nag.

Our poesy is a gum, which oozes from whence 'tis nourish'd. A thing slipp'd idly from me. The fire i' th' flint shows not till it be struck. Our gentle flame provokes itself and like the current flies each bound it chafes, flies an eagle flight, bold and forth on leaving no tract behind. Much is the force of heaven-bred poesy. The poet's eye, in a fine frenzy rolling, doth glance from heaven to earth, from earth to heaven; and as imagination bodies forth the forms of things unknown, the poet's pen turns them to shapes, and gives to airy nothing a local habitation and a name. Never durst poet touch a pen to write until his ink were temp'red with Love's sighs. . . . Then his lines would ravish savage ears and plant in tyrants mild humility.

Who will believe my verse in time to come if it were fill'd with your most high deserts? Though yet, heaven knows, it is but as a tomb which hides your life and shows not half your parts. If I could write the beauty of your eyes and in fresh numbers number all your graces, the age to come would say, "This poet lies! Such heavenly touches ne'er touch'd earthly faces." When in the chronicle of wasted time I see descriptions of the fairest wights, and beauty making beautiful old rhyme in praise of ladies dead and lovely knights, then, in the blazon of sweet beauty's best, of hand, of foot, of lip, of eye, of brow, I see their antique pen would have express'd even such a beauty as you master now. So all their praises are but prophecies of this our time, all you pre-figuring; and, for they look'd but with divining eyes, they had not skill enough your worth to sing. But you shall shine more bright in these contents than unswept stone, besmear'd with sluttish time. When time is old and hath forgot itself, when water drops have worn the stones of Troy, and blind oblivion swallow'd cities up, and mighty states characterless are grated to dusty noth-ing, when wasteful war shall statues overturn, and broils root out the work of masonry, nor Mars his sword nor war's quick fire shall burn the living record of your memory. 'Gainst death and all-oblivious enmity shall

[67]

you pace forth; your praise shall still find room even in the eyes of all posterity that wear this world out to the ending doom. Not marble nor the gilded monuments of princes shall outlive this pow'rful rhyme.

Reputation and Slander

THE purest treasure mortal times afford is spotless reputation. That away, men are but gilded loam or painted clay. Good name in man and woman . . . is the immediate jewel of their souls. Who steals my purse steals trash; 'tis something, nothing; 'twas mine, 'tis his, and has been slave to thousands; but he that filches from me my good name robs me of that which not enriches him and makes me poor indeed.

Be thou as chaste as ice, as pure as snow, thou shalt not escape calumny. Virtue itself scapes not calumnious strokes, for calumny will sear virtue itself. No might nor greatness in mortality can censure scape. Back-wounding calumny the whitest virtue strikes. What king so strong can tie the gall up in the slanderous tongue?

'Tis slander, whose edge is sharper than the sword, whose tongue outvenoms all the worms of Nile, whose breath rides on the posting winds and doth belie all corners of the world, slander whose whisper o'er the world's diameter . . . transports his poison'd shot. Kings, queens, and states, maids, matrons, nay, the secrets of the grave this viperous slander enters. For slander lives upon succession, forever housed where it gets possession.

Rumour is a pipe blown by surmises, jealousies, conjectures; and of so easy and so plain a stop that the blunt monster with uncounted heads, the still-discordant wav'ring multitude, can play upon it.

On Opportunity

→»«←

WHO seeks, and will not take when once 'tis offer'd, shall
never find it more. There is a tide in the affairs of men
which, taken at the flood, leads on to fortune; omitted,
all the voyage of their life is bound in shallows and in
miseries. On such a full sea are we now afloat, and we
must take the current when it serves or lose our ventures.
Embrace we then this opportunity; if once it be neg-
lected, ten to one we shall not find like opportunity.
Let's take the instant by the forward top ... on our
quick'st decrees th' inaudible and noiseless foot of Time
steals, ere we can effect them.

O opportunity, thy guilt is great! 'Tis thou that
execut'st the traitor's treason; thou sett'st the wolf where
he the lamb may get; whoever plots the sin, thou point'st
the season. 'Tis thou that spurn'st at right, at law, at
reason; and in thy shady cell, where none may spy him,
sits Sin, to seize the souls that wander by him. Thou
makest the vestal violate her oath; thou blowest the fire
when temperance is thaw'd; thou smother'st honesty,
thou murth'rest troth; thou foul abettor! Thou notorious bawd! Thou plantest scandal and displacest laud.
Thou ravisher, thou traitor, thou false thief! Thy honey
turns to gall. . . . Thy secret pleasure turns to open
shame, thy private feasting to a public fast, thy smooth-

ing titles to a ragged name . . . thy violent vanities can never, never last.

When wilt thou be the humble suppliant's friend? . . . When wilt thou sort an hour great strifes to end? Or free that soul which wretchedness hath chained? Give physic to the sick, ease to the pained? The poor, lame, blind, halt, creep, cry out for thee; but they ne'er meet with Opportunity. The patient dies while the physician sleeps; the orphan pines while the oppressor feeds; justice is feasting while the widow weeps; advice is sporting while infection breeds. Thou grant'st no time for charitable deeds: wrath, envy, treason, rape, and murther's rages, thy heinous hours wait on them as their pages. When Truth and Virtue have to do with thee, a thousand crosses keep them from thy aid. They buy thy help; but Sin ne'er gives a fee, he gratis comes. . . . Guilty thou art of murther and of theft, guilty of perjury and subornation, guilty of treason, forgery, and shift, guilty of incest . . . an accessary by thine inclination to all sins past and all that are to come, from the creation to the general doom.

Of the Virtue of Action

→→»«←←

MAN—how dearly ever parted, how much in having, or
without or in—cannot make boast to have that which he
hath, nor feels not what he owes, but by reflection; as
when his virtues aiming upon others, heat them and they
retort that heat again to the first giver.

There is a kind of character in thy life that to th'
observer doth thy history fully unfold. Thyself and thy
belongings are not thine own so proper as to waste thyself upon thy virtues, they on thee. Heaven doth with
us as we with torches do, not light them for themselves;
for if our virtues did not go forth of us, 'twere all alike
as if we had them not. Spirits are not finely touch'd but
to fine issues; nor Nature never lends the smallest scruple
of her excellence but, like a thrifty goddess, she determines herself the glory of a creditor, both thanks and
use.

This is not strange. . . . The beauty that is borne here
in the face the bearer knows not, but commends itself
to others' eyes; nor doth the eye itself, that most pure
spirit of sense, behold itself, not going from itself; but
eye to eye oppos'd salutes each other with each other's
form; for speculation turns not to itself, till it hath
travel'd and is mirror'd there where it may see itself.
This is not strange at all. . . . It is familiar. . . . No man

[73]

is the lord of anything, though in and of him there is much consisting, till he communicate his parts to others; nor doth he of himself know them for aught till he behold them formed in th' applause where th' are extended, who, like an arch, reverb'rate the voice again, or, like a gate of steel fronting the sun, receives and renders back his figure and his heat.

Of Ingratitude

⇢⇥≪⇠

SEE the monstrousness of man when he looks out in an ungrateful shape. I hate ingratitude more in a man than lying, vainness, babbling, drunkenness, or any taint of any vice whose strong corruption inhabits our frail blood. Old fellows have their ingratitude in them hereditary. Their blood is cak'd, 'tis cold, it seldom flows. 'Tis lack of kindly warmth they are not kind; and nature, as it grows again toward earth, is fashion'd for the journey, dull and heavy. Ingratitude is monstrous. Ingratitude, thou marble-hearted fiend, more hideous when thou showest thee in a child, than the sea-monster! Sharper than a serpent's tooth it is to have a thankless child. Filial ingratitude! Is it not as this mouth should tear this hand for lifting food to 't?

Common mother, thou whose womb unmeasurable and infinite breast . . . whereof thy proud child, arrogant man, is puff'd, engenders the black toad and adder blue, the gilded newt and eyeless venom'd worm, with all the abhorred births below crisp heaven whereon Hyperion's quick'ning fire doth shine . . . ensear thy fertile and conceptious womb; let it no more bring out ingrateful man! Go great with tigers, dragons, wolves, and bears; teem with new monsters whom thy upward face hath to the marbled mansion all above never presented! Blow,

[75]

winds, and crack your cheeks! rage! blow! you cataracts and hurricanoes, spout till you have drench'd our steeples, drown'd the cocks! You sulph'rous and thought-executing fires, vaunt-couriers to oak-cleaving thunderbolts, singe my white head! And thou, all-shaking thunder, strike flat the thick rotundity o' th' world, crack Nature's moulds, all germains spill at once, that make ungrateful man.

Of Politics and Politicians

-》》《《-

POLICY sits above conscience. Conscience is a word that cowards use, devis'd at first to keep the strong in awe. I'll not meddle with it ... it makes a man a coward. A man cannot steal, but it accuseth him; a man cannot swear, but it checks him; a man cannot lie with his neighbour's wife, but it detects him. 'Tis a blushing shamefac'd spirit that mutinies in a man's bosom. It fills a man full of obstacles. . . . It beggars any man that keeps it. It is turn'd out of towns and cities for a dangerous thing, and every man that means to live well endeavours to trust to himself and lives without it.

They tax our policy and call it cowardice, count wisdom as no member of the war, forestall prescience, and esteem no act but that of hand. The still and mental parts, that do contrive how many hands shall strike when fitness calls them on, and know by measure of their observant toil the enemies' weight—why, this hath not a finger's dignity! They call this bedwork, mapp'ry, closet war: so that the ram that batters down the wall, for the great swinge and rudeness of his poise, they place before his hand that made the engine or those that with the fineness of their souls by reason guide his execution. The providence that's in a watchful state, knows almost every grain of Pluto's gold; finds bottom in th' uncomprehen-

[77]

sive depth; keeps place with thought, and almost, like the gods, does thoughts unveil in their dumb cradles. There is a mystery (with whom relation durst never meddle) in the soul of state, which hath an operation more divine than breath or pen can give expressure to.

Plague of your policy! Policy I hate, that same purpose-changer, that sly devil, that broker that still breaks the pate of faith, that daily break-vow, he that wins of all, of kings, of beggars, old men, young men, maids . . . that smoothfac'd gentleman. . . . Commodity, the bias of the world—the world, who of itself is peized well, made to run even upon even ground till this advantage, this vile drawing bias, this sway of motion, this Commodity, makes it take head from all indifferency, from all direction, purpose, course, intent. The devil knew not what he did when he made man politic. He crossed himself by't; and I cannot think but, in the end, the villanies of man will set him clear.

There's no art to find the mind's construction in the face. When my outward action doth demonstrate the native act and figure of my heart in compliment extern, 'tis not long after but I will wear my heart upon my sleeve for daws to peck at. I . . . seem a saint when most I play the devil. Look like the innocent flower, but be the serpent under't. I'll drown more sailors than the mermaid shall; I'll slay more gazers than the basilisk; I'll play the orator as well as Nestor, deceive more slily than Ulysses could, and, like a Sinon, take another Troy. 'Tis the sport to have the enginer hoist with his own petard. I can add colours to the chameleon, change shapes with

[78]

Proteus for advantages, and set the murtherous Machiavel to school. Nor sleep nor sanctuary, being naked, sick, nor fane nor Capitol, the prayers of priests nor times of sacrifice, embargements all of fury, shall lift up their rotten privilege and custom 'gainst my hate. Tut, I have done a thousand dreadful things as willingly as one would kill a fly; and nothing grieves me heartily indeed but that I cannot do ten thousand more.

Yet, to avoid deceit, I mean to learn; for it shall strew the footsteps of my rising. Am I politic? Am I subtle? Am I a Machiavel?

Of War

>>><<<

SHALL we at last conclude effeminate peace? Peace is nothing but to rust iron, increase tailors and breed ballad-makers. . . . Peace is a very apoplexy, lethargy; mull'd, deaf, sleepy, insensible; a getter of more bastard children than war's a destroyer of men. . . . Ay, and it makes men hate one another. And quietness, grown sick of rest, would purge by any desperate change. Plenty and peace breeds cowards. I, in this weak piping time of peace, have no delight to pass away the time. Therefore . . . busy giddy minds with foreign quarrels.

In peace there's nothing so becomes a man as modest stillness and humility; but when the blast of war blows in our ears, then imitate the action of the tiger: stiffen the sinews, summon up the blood, disguise fair nature with hard-favour'd rage; then lend the eye a terrible aspect; let it pry through the portage of the head like the brass cannon; let the brow o'erwhelm it as fearfully as doth a galled rock o'erhang and jutty his confounded base, swill'd with the wild and wasteful ocean. Now set the teeth and stretch the nostril wide, hold hard the breath and bend up every spirit to his full height! . . . Be copy now to men of grosser blood and teach them how to war! The gates of mercy shall be all shut up, and the flesh'd soldier, rough and hard of heart, in liberty of bloody hand shall range with conscience wide as hell, mowing like grass your fresh fair virgins and your flow'ring infants. What is it then to me if impious war, array'd in flames like to the prince of fiends, do with his smirch'd complexion all fell feats enlink'd to waste and desolation? What is't to me, when you yourselves are cause, if your pure maidens fall into the hand of hot and forcing violation? What rein can hold licentious wickedness when down the hill he holds his fierce career? We may as bootless spend our vain command upon th' enraged soldiers in their spoil as send precepts to the Leviathan to come ashore.

World, thou hast a pair of chaps, ... and throw between them all the food thou hast, they'll grind the one the other. Now for the bare-pick'd bone of majesty doth dogged war bristle his angry crest and snarleth in the gentle eyes of peace, now powers from home and discontents at home meet in one line; and vast confusion waits, as doth a raven on a sick-fall'n beast, the imminent decay of wrested pomp. Now doth Death line his dead chaps with steel; the swords of soldiers are his teeth, his fangs; and now he feasts, mousing the flesh of men in undetermin'd differences.

Whose powers are these? ... how purpos'd? ... Truly to speak ... to gain a little patch of ground that hath in it no profit but the name. To pay five ducats, five, I would not farm it. ... Two thousand souls and twenty thousand ducats will not debate the question of this straw. Look on fertile France, and see the cities and towns defac'd by wasting ruin of the cruel foe. Now do I prophesy ... a curse shall light upon the limbs of men;

domestic fury and fierce civil strife shall cumber all the parts of Italy; blood and destruction shall be so in use and dreadful objects so familiar that mothers shall but smile when they behold their infants quartered with the hands of war, all pity chok'd with custom of fell deeds; and Caesar's spirit, ranging for revenge, with Ate by his side come hot from hell, shall in these confines with a monarch's voice cry 'Havoc!' and let slip the dogs of war, that this foul deed shall smell above the earth with carrion men, groaning for burial.

Of Peace

>>>-<<<

WHEREFORE do you so ill translate yourself out of speech
of peace, that bears such grace, into the harsh and bois-
t'rous tongue of war; turning your books to graves, your
ink to blood, your pens to lances, and your tongue
divine to a loud trumpet and a point of war? Thy
threat'ning colours now wind up and tame the savage
spirit of wild war, that, like a lion fostered up at hand,
it may lie gently at the foot of peace. A peace is of the
nature of a conquest; for then both parties nobly are
subdu'd, and neither party loser. Peace, dear nurse of
arts, plenty and joyful births. Enrich the time to come
with smooth-fac'd peace, with smiling plenty, and fair
prosperous days! Piety and fear, religion to the gods,
peace, justice, truth, domestic awe, night-rest and neigh-
bourhood, instruction, manners, mysteries and trades.
And sing the merry songs of peace to all neighbours, our
tradesmen singing in their shops and going about their
functions friendly; peace should still her wheaten garland wear. The time of universal peace is near ... the
three-nook'd world shall bear the olive freely.

Peace itself should not so dull a kingdom ... but that
defences, musters, preparations should be maintain'd.

Of Nature

→>X<←

IN NATURE'S infinite book of secrecy a little I can read. And I can speak of the disturbances that nature works, and of her cures; which doth give me a more content in course of true delight than to be thirsty after tottering honour, or tie my treasure up in silken bags, to please the fool and death. By turning o'er authorities, I have, together with my practice, made familiar to me and to my aid the blest infusions that dwell in vegetives, in metals, stones, many for many virtues excellent, none but for some, and yet all different. O, mickle is the powerful grace that lies in plants, herbs, stones, and their true qualities. Diseased nature oftentimes breaks forth in strange eruptions; oft the teeming earth is with a kind of colic pinch'd and vex'd by the imprisoning of unruly wind within her womb, which, for enlargement striving, shakes the old beldame earth and topples down steeples and mossgrown towers: Death may usurp on nature many hours, and yet the fire of life kindle again the o'erpress'd spirits. I heard of an Egyptian that had nine hours lien dead, who was by good appliance recovered.

Nature's above art, whose end, both at the first and now, was and is, to hold, as 'twere, the mirror up to nature; labouring art can never ransom nature from her inaidable estate. To gild refined gold, to paint the lily, to throw a perfume on the violet, to smooth the ice, or add another hue unto the rainbow, or with taper light to seek the beauteous eye of heaven to garnish, is wasteful and ridiculous excess. I have heard it said there is an art which . . . shares with great creating nature. . . . Yet nature is made better by no mean but nature makes that mean. So, over that art which you say adds to nature, is an art that nature makes. . . . We marry a gentler scion to the wildest stock and make conceive a bark of baser kind by bud of nobler race. This is an art which does mend nature—change it rather; but the art itself is nature.

It is the show and seal of nature's truth where love's strong passion is impress'd in youth. Nature is fine in love, and where 'tis fine, it sends some precious instance of itself after the thing it loves. Base men being in love have then a nobility in their natures more than is native to them.

If Nature (sovereign mistress over wrack), as thou goest onwards, still will pluck thee back, she keeps thee to this purpose, that her skill may time disgrace, and wretched minutes kill. Yet fear her, O thou minion of her pleasure! She may detain, but not still keep, her treasure; her audit, though delay'd, answer'd must be, and her quietus is to render thee. When Nature calls thee to be gone, what acceptable audit canst thou leave? Nature never lends the smallest scruple of her excellence but, like a thrifty goddess, she determines herself the glory of a creditor, both thanks and use. Thou, Nature, art my goddess; to thy law my services are bound.

[85]

On the Force of Custom

->>><<-

NATURE her custom holds. What custom wills, in all things should we do it, the dust on antique time would lie unswept and mountainous error be too highly heaped for truth to overpeer. We must not make a scarecrow of the law, setting it up to fear the birds of prey, and let it keep one shape till custom make it their perch, and not their terror. New customs, though they be never so ridiculous . . . yet are follow'd. That monster, custom, who all sense doth eat of habits evil, is angel yet in this, that to the use of actions fair and good he likewise gives a frock or livery, that aptly is put on. Refrain to-night and that shall lend a kind of easiness to the next abstinence; the next more easy; for use almost can change the stamp of nature, and master ev'n the devil, or throw him out with wondrous potency.

Back to Nature

-»»×««-

WHEN Jove will o'er some high-vic'd city hang his poison in the sick air, unfrequented woods I better brook
than flourishing peopled towns, cities that of Plenty's
cup and her prosperities so largely taste, with their
superfluous riots. Did you but know the city's usuries
and felt them knowingly; the art o' th' court, as hard
to leave as keep, whose top to climb is certain falling,
or so slipp'ry that the fear is as bad as falling; the toil
of th' war, a pain that only seems to seek out danger, i'
th' name of fame and honour, which dies i' th' search
and hath as oft a sland'rous epitaph as record of fair
act, [you would] to the woods where [you would] find
the unkindest beast kinder than mankind. Are not
these woods more free from peril than the envious
court? Here feel we but the penalty of Adam, the season's difference; as, the icy fang and churlish chiding
of the winter's wind, which, when it bites and blows
upon my body, even till I shrink with cold, I smile
and say, "This is no flattery; these are counsellors
that feelingly persuade me what I am." . . . This our
life, exempt from public haunt, finds tongues in trees,
books in the running brooks, sermons in stones, and
good in everything.

Plenty and peace breed cowards; hardness ever of

hardiness is mother. . . . Weariness can snore upon the flint when resty sloth finds the down pillow hard. Let the superfluous and lust-dieted man, . . . that will not see because he does not feel, feel . . . quickly; so distribution should undo excess, and each man have enough.

Why should you want? Behold the earth hath roots; within this mile break forth a hundred springs; the oaks bear mast, the briars scarlet hips; the bounteous housewife Nature on each bush lays her full mess before you. Want? Why want?

Had I plantation . . . i' the commonwealth, I would by contraries execute all things; for no kind of traffic would I admit; no name of magistrate; letters should not be known; riches, poverty, and use of service, none; contract, succession, bourn, bound of land, tilth, vineyard, none; no use of metal, corn, or wine, or oil; no occupation; all men idle, all; and women too, but innocent and pure; no sovereignty. . . . All things in common nature should produce without sweat or endeavor. Treason, felony, sword, pike, knife, gun, or need of any engine would I not have; but nature should bring forth, of its own kind, all foison, all abundance, to feed my innocent people. . . . I would with such perfection govern . . . t' excel the golden age.

On the Nature of Man

->>)«<-

O THE difference of man and man! All men are not alike; clay and clay differs in dignity, whose dust is both alike. In the catalogue ye go for men, as hounds and greyhounds, mongrels, spaniels, curs, shoughs, water-rugs, and demi-wolves are clept all by the name of dogs. The valued file distinguishes the swift, the slow, the subtle, the housekeeper, the hunter, every one according to the gift which bounteous nature has in him clos'd; whereby he does receive particular addition, from the bill that writes them all alike; and so of men. In the reproof of chance lies the true proof of men, the protractive trials of great Jove to find persistive constancy in men; the fineness of which metal is not found in Fortune's love; for then the bold and coward, the wise and fool, the artist and unread, the hard and soft, seem all affin'd and kin. But in the wind and tempest of her frown distinction, with a broad and pow'rful fan, puffing at all, winnows the light away, and what hath mass or matter, by itself lies rich in virtue and unmingled.

Will you tell me . . . how to choose a man? Care I for the limb, the thews, the stature, bulk, and big assemblance of a man? Give me the spirit. . . . Is not birth, beauty, good shape, discourse, manhood, learning, gen-

[89]

tleness, virtue, youth, liberality, and such-like, the spice and salt that season a man?

What a piece of work is a man! how noble in reason! how infinite in faculties! in form and moving how express and admirable! in action how like an angel! in apprehension how like a god! the beauty of the world, the paragon of animals! And yet to me what is this quintessence of dust? We must think men are not gods. A noble nature may catch a wrench. Correction and instruction must both work ere this rude beast will profit. In men, as in a rough-grown grove, remain cave-keeping evils that obscurely sleep. Virtue cannot so inoculate our old stock but we shall relish of it.

We profess ourselves to be the slaves of chance and flies of every wind that blows. Were man but constant, he were perfect! That one error fills him with faults, makes him run through all th' sins. Our natures do pursue, like rats that ravin down their proper bane, a thirsty evil, and when we drink we die. I wonder men dare trust themselves with men! Thou almost mak'st me waver in my faith, to hold opinion with Pythagoras, that souls of animals infuse themselves into the trunks of men. There's nothing level in our cursed natures but direct villainy. What! are men mad? Hath nature given them eyes to see this vaulted arch and the rich crop of sea and land, which can distinguish 'twixt the fiery orbs above, and the twinn'd stones upon th' unnumber'd beach, and can we not partition make with spectacles so precious 'twixt fair and foul?

Of the Beast in Man

>>><<<

WHAT is a man, if his chief good and market of his time be but to sleep and feed? A beast, no more. Sure he that made us with such large discourse, looking before and after, gave us not that capability and godlike reason, to fust in us unused. Divided from . . . fair judgment . . . we are pictures or mere beasts, fox in stealth, wolf in greediness, dog in madness, lion in prey. You may as well go stand upon the beach and bid the main flood bate his usual height; you may as well use question with the wolf, why he hath made the ewe bleat for the lamb; you may as well forbid the mountain pines to wag their high tops and to make no noise when they are fretten with the gusts of heaven; you may as well do anything most hard as seek to soften . . . his heart. The strain of man's bred out into babboon and monkey. Man, proud man, drest in a little brief authority, most ignorant of what he's most assured, his glassy essence, like an angry ape, plays such fantastic tricks before high heaven as make the angels weep.

Wouldst thou have thyself fall in the confusion of men, and remain a beast with the beasts? . . . If thou wert the lion, the fox would beguile thee. If thou wert the lamb, the fox would eat thee. If thou wert the fox, the lion would suspect thee, when peradventure thou

[91]

wert accus'd by the ass. If thou wert the ass, thy dulness would torment thee, and still thou liv'dst but as a breakfast to the wolf. If thou wert the wolf, thy greediness would afflict thee, and oft thou shouldst hazard thy life for thy dinner. Wert thou the unicorn, pride and wrath would confound thee and make thine own self the conquest of thy fury. Wert thou a bear, thou wouldst be kill'd by the horse; wert thou a horse, thou wouldst be seiz'd by the leopard; wert thou a leopard, thou wert german to the lion, and the spots of thy kindred were jurors on thy life. . . . What beast couldst thou be that were not subject to a beast? And what a beast art thou already, that seest not thy loss in transformation! . . . The commonwealth of Athens is become a forest of beasts.

Of a Perfect Man

→»)«←

HE WAS a man, take him for all in all, I shall not look upon his like again; the courtier's, scholar's, soldier's eye, tongue, sword, th' expectancy and rose of the fair state, the glass of fashion and the mould of form, th' observ'd of all observers. A sweeter and a lovelier gentleman—fram'd in the prodigality of nature, young, valiant, wise . . . right royal—the spacious world cannot again afford; the front of Jove himself; an eye like Mars, to threaten and command; a station like the herald Mercury new lighted on a heaven-kissing hill: a combination and a form indeed where every god did seem to set his seal to give the world assurance of a man. He would not flatter Neptune for his trident or Jove for 's power to thunder. For his bounty, there was no winter in it; in bestowing . . . he was most princely. Ever witness for him those twins of learning he raised . . . Ipswich and Oxford; one of which fell with him, unwilling to outlive the good that did it; the other, though unfinish'd, yet so famous, so excellent in art, and still so rising, that Christendom shall ever speak his virtue.

Contempt nor bitterness were in his pride or sharpness. If they were, his equal had awaked them, and his honour, clock to itself, knew the true minute when ex-

[93]

ception bid him speak, and at this time his tongue obey'd his hand. Who were below him he us'd as creatures of another place; and bow'd his eminent top to their low ranks, making them proud of his humility, in their poor praise he humbled. Such a man might be a copy to these younger times, which followed well, would demonstrate them now but goers backward. One, in suff'ring all, that suffers nothing; a man that Fortune's buffets and rewards hast ta'en with equal thanks; and blest are those whose blood and judgment are so well commingled that they are not a pipe for Fortune's finger to sound what stop she please. Give me that man that is not passion's slave, and I will wear him in my heart of hearts.

Nothing in his life became him like the leaving it. He died as one that had been studied in his death to throw away the dearest thing he ow'd as 'twere a careless trifle. His overthrow heap'd happiness upon him; for then, and not till then, he felt himself and found the blessedness of being little. And, to add greater honours to his age than man could give him, he died fearing God. His life was gentle, and the elements so mix'd in him that Nature might stand up and say to all the world, "This was a man!"

A Most Imperfect Man

-->>><<<-

A SLAVE whom Fortune's tender arm with favour never clasp'd, but bred a dog. Hadst thou . . . proceeded the sweet degrees that this brief world affords to such as may the passive drudges of it freely command, thou wouldst have plung'd thyself in general riot, melted down thy youth in different beds of lust, and never learn'd the icy precepts of respect, but followed the sugar'd game before thee; swore as many oaths as . . . spake words, and broke them in the sweet face of heaven; . . . wine lov'd . . . deeply, dice dearly; and in woman out-paramour'd the Turk. False of heart, light of ear, bloody of hand.

He will steal . . . an egg out of a cloister. For rapes and ravishments he parallels Nesus. He professes not keeping of oaths; in breaking 'em he is stronger than Hercules. He will lie . . . with such volubility that you would think truth were a fool. Drunkenness is his best virtue, for he will be swine-drunk, and in his sleep he does little harm, save to his bedclothes about him; but they know his conditions and lay him in straw. I have but little more to say . . . of his honesty. He has everything that an honest man should not have; what an honest man should have, he has nothing.

A stubborn soul that apprehends life no further than

this world, and squar'st life according; an inhuman wretch, uncapable of pity, void and empty from any dram of mercy; a notorious liar . . . great way fool, solely a coward; an hourly promise breaker, the owner of no one good quality; a wretch whom nature is asham'd almost t' acknowledge hers; such smiling rogues, . . . like rats, oft bite the holy cords atwain that are too intrinse t' unloose; smooth every passion that in the natures of their lords rebel, bring oil to fire, snow to their colder moods; renege, affirm, and turn their halcyon beaks with every gale and vary of their masters, knowing nought (like dogs) but following.

A knave, a rascal; an eater of broken meats; a base, proud, shallow, beggarly, three-suited, hundred-pound, filthy, worsted-stocking knave; a lily-liver'd, action-taking, whoreson, glass-gazing, superserviceable, finical rogue; one-trunk-inheriting slave; one that wouldst be a bawd in way of good service, and art nothing but the composition of a knave, beggar, coward, pander, and the son and heir of a mongrel bitch.

A Perfect Woman

➔➤✕◆

ONE woman is fair, yet I am well; another is wise, yet I am well; another virtuous, yet I am well; but till all graces be in one woman, one woman shall not come in my grace. Rich she shall be, that's certain; wise, or I'll none; virtuous, or I'll never cheapen her; fair or I'll never look on her; mild or come not near me; noble, or not I for an angel; of good discourse, an excellent musician and her hair shall be of what color it please God. Full many a lady I have ey'd with best regard, and many a time th' harmony of their tongues hath into bondage brought my too diligent ear; for several virtues have I lik'd several woman; never any with so full soul but some defect in her did quarrel with the noblest grace she ow'd and put it to the foil; but you . . . so perfect and so peerless, are created of every creature's best!

She's fair and royal, and . . . she hath all courtly parts more exquisite than lady, ladies, woman. From every one the best she hath, and she, of all compounded, outsells them all. The senate house of planets all did sit to knit in her their best perfections. She excels each mortal thing upon the dull earth dwelling, a lady, wiser, fairer, truer than ever Greek did compass in his arms, whose youth and freshness wrinkles Apollo's and makes stale the morning, with a mind that doth renew swifter than blood decays. Why if two gods should play some heavenly match, and on the wager lay two earthly women . . . there must be something else pawn'd with the other; for the poor rude world hath not her fellow. Falseness cannot come from thee; for thou lookest modest as Justice, and thou seem'st a palace for the crown'd truth to dwell in.

An Imperfect Woman

SHE's the kitchen wench, and all grease; and I know not what use to put her to but to make a lamp of her and run from her by her own light. I warrant, her rags and the tallow in them will burn a Poland winter. If she lives till doomsday, she'll burn a week longer than the whole world. . . . Swart like my shoe, but her face nothing like so clean kept: for why, she sweats; a man may go over shoes in the grime of it. . . . No longer from head to foot than from hip to hip. She is spherical, like a globe. I could find countries in her. . . . Ireland? . . . In her buttocks. I found it out by the bogs. . . . Scotland? I found by the barrenness, hard in the palm of the hand. Where France? In her forehead arm'd and reverted, making war against her heir. . . . England? I look'd for the chalky cliffs, but I could find no whiteness in them. But I guess it stood in her chin by the salt rheum that ran between France and it. . . . Spain? Faith! I saw it not; but I felt it hot in her breath. . . . America, the Indies? . . . Upon her nose, all o'er embellished with rubies, carbuncles, sapphires, declining their rich aspect to the hot breath of Spain, who sent whole armadoes of carracks to be ballast at her nose. . . . Belgia, the Netherlands? . . . I did not look so low. She speaks poniards, and every word stabs. If her breath were as terrible as her terminations, there were no living near her; she would infect to the North Star. I would not marry her though she were endowed with all that Adam had left him before he transgress'd. She would have made Hercules turn's spit, yes, and have cleft his club to make the fire too. . . . You shall find her the infernal Ate in good apparel. I would to God some scholar would conjure her, for certainly, while she is here, a man may live as quiet in hell as in sanctuary; and people sin upon purpose, because they would go thither; so indeed all disquiet, horror, and perturbation follow her.

Anybody's Woman

→»«←

WHO is't can read a woman? This woman's an easy glove . . . she goes off and on at pleasure. Every inch of woman in the world, ay, every dram of woman's flesh is false. Frailty, thy name is woman! God hath given you one face, and you make yourselves another. You jig, you amble, and you lisp, and nickname God's creatures and make your wantonness your ignorance. He's mad that trusts in the tameness of a wolf, a horse's health, a boy's love, or a whore's oath. You are not oathable, although I know you'll swear, terribly swear into strong shudders and to heavenly agues th' immortal gods that hear you. Spare your oaths. The wiles and guiles that women work, dissembled with an outward show, the tricks and toys that in them lurk, the cock that treads them shall not know.

Proper deformity seems not in the fiend so horrid as in woman. Behold yond simp'ring dame, whose face between her forks presageth snow, that minces virtue, and does shake the head to hear of pleasure's name. The fitchew nor the soiled horse goes to't with a more riotous appetite. Down from the waist they are Centaurs, though women all above. But to the girdle do the gods inherit, beneath is all the fiends. There's hell, there's darkness, there's the sulphurous pit; burning,

[101]

scalding, stench, consumption. . . . Give me an ounce of civet, good apothecary, to sweeten my imagination.

O indistinguish'd space of woman's will! There's no motion that tends to vice in man but I affirm it is the woman's part. Be it lying, note it, the woman's; flattering, hers; deceiving, hers; lust and rank thoughts, hers, hers; revenges, hers; ambitions, coveting, change of prides, disdain, nice longing, slanders, mutability—all faults that may be nam'd, nay, that hell knows, why, hers, in part or all; but rather all! For even to vice they are not constant, but are changing still one vice but of a minute old for one not half so old as that. What woman in the city do I name when that I say the city woman bears the cost of princes on unworthy shoulders. There's language in her eye, her cheek, her lip; nay, her foot speaks. Her wanton spirits look out at every joint and motive of her body. O, these encounterers so glib of tongue, that give accosting welcome ere it comes and wide unclasp the tables of their thoughts to every ticklish reader—set them down for sluttish spoils of opportunity and daughters of the game!

On Virginity

->>)«<-

ARE you meditating on virginity? It is not politic in
the commonwealth of nature to preserve virginity.
Virginity being blown down, man will quicklier be
blown up. Marry, in blowing him down again, with the
breach yourselves made you lose your city. Loss of virginity is rational increase; and there was never virgin
got till virginity was first lost. That you were made of
is metal to make virgins. Virginity by being once lost
may be ten times found; by being ever kept it is ever
lost. 'Tis too cold a companion. Away with 't.

There's little can be said in't; 'tis against the rule of
nature. To speak on the part of virginity is to accuse
your mothers, which is most infallible disobedience.
He that hangs himself is a virgin: virginity murthers
itself, and should be buried in highways out of all
sanctified limit, as a desperate offendress against nature. Virginity breeds mites, much like a cheese; con-
sumes itself to the very paring, and so dies with feeding
his own stomach. Besides, virginity is peevish, proud,
idle, made of self-love, which is the most inhibited sin
in the canon. Keep it not; you cannot choose but lose
by 't. Out with 't! within the year it will make itself
two, which is a goodly increase, and the principal itself
not much the worse. Away with 't. . . .

[103]

'Tis a commodity will lose the gloss with lying; the longer kept, the less worth. Off with 't while 'tis vendible; answer the time of request. Virginity, like an old courtier, wears her cap out of fashion; richly suited, but unsuitable: just like the brooch and the toothpick, which wear not now. Your date is better in your pie and your porridge than in your cheek; and your virginity, your old virginity, is like one of our French wither'd pears; it looks ill, it eats drily. Marry, 'tis a wither'd pear; it was formerly better; marry, yet 'tis a wither'd pear! Will you anything with it?

Some Strange Fellows

>>>x<<<-

NATURE hath fram'd strange fellows in her time: some that will evermore peep through their eyes, and laugh like parrots at a bagpiper; and other of such vinegar aspect that they'll not show their teeth in way of smile, though Nestor swear the jest be laughable. Some men there are love not a gaping pig, some that are mad if they behold a cat, and others, when the bagpipe sings i' th' nose, cannot contain their urine; for affection, mistress of passion, sways it to the mood of what it likes or loathes. Who would believe that there were mountaineers dewlapp'd like bulls, whose throats had hanging at 'em wallets of flesh? or that there were such men whose heads stood in their breasts? I knew a man of eighty winters . . . who a lass of fourteen brided. . . . The aged cramp had screw'd his square foot round, the gout had knit his fingers into knots; torturing convulsions from his globy eyes had almost drawn their spheres, that what was life in him seem'd torture. This anatomy had by his young fair feere a boy.

There is the Neapolitan prince . . . a colt indeed, for he doth nothing but talk of his horse; and he makes it a great appropriation to his own good parts that he can shoe him himself. I am much afear'd my lady, his mother, play'd false with a smith. Then is there the

County Palatine. He doth nothing but frown; as who should say, 'An you will not have me, choose!' He hears merry tales and smiles not. I fear he will prove the weeping philosopher when he grows old, being so full of unmannerly sadness in his youth.... The French Lord, Monsieur Le Bon? God made him, and therefore let him pass for a man. In truth, I know it is a sin to be a mocker; but he—why, he hath a horse better than the Neopolitan's, a better bad habit of frowning than the Count Palatine. He is every man in no man. If a throstle sing, he falls straight a-cap'ring; he will fence with his own shadow. Falconbridge, the young baron of England? ... He hath neither Latin, French, nor Italian; and you will come into court and swear that I have a poor pennyworth in the English. He is a proper man's picture; but alas! who can converse with a dumb-show? How oddly he is suited! I think he bought his doublet in Italy, his round hose in France, his bonnet in Germany, and his behaviour everywhere.... The Scottish lord, his neighbour? ... He hath a neighbourly charity in him; for he borrowed a box of the ear of the Englishman, and swore he would pay him again when he was able. I think the Frenchman became his surety and seal'd under for another.... The young German, the Duke of Saxony's nephew? ... When he is best, he is a little worse than a man; and when he is worst he is little better than a beast.

This man ... hath robb'd many beasts of their particular additions. He is as valiant as the lion, churlish as the bear, slow as the elephant; a man into whom nature hath so crowded humours that his valour is crush'd

[106]

into folly, his folly sauced with discretion. There is no man hath a virtue that he hath not a glimpse of, nor any man an attaint but he carries some stain of it. He is melancholy without cause and merry against the hair. He hath the joints of everything, but everything so out of joint that he is a gouty Briareus, many hands and no use, or purblind Argus, all eyes and no sight. Faith, here's a gull, a fool, a rogue, that now and then goes to the wars to grace himself at his return to London under the form of a soldier. And such fellows are perfect in the great commanders' names, and they will learn you by rote where services were done:—at such and such a sconce, at such a breach, at such a convoy; who came off bravely, who was shot, who disgrac'd, what terms the enemy stood on; and this they con perfectly in the phase of war, which they trick up with new-tuned oaths; and what a beard of the General's cut and a horrid suit of the camp will do among foaming bottles and ale-wash'd wits is wonderful to be thought on. [Here's] a serving-man, proud in heart and mind; that curl'd hair, wore gloves in . . . cap; serv'd the lust of his mistress' heart and did the act of darkness with her; swore as many oaths as . . . spake words, and broke them in the sweet face of heaven; one that slept in the contriving of lust, and wak'd to do it.

The country gives . . . proof and precedent of Bedlam beggars, who, with roaring voices, strike in their numb'd and mortified bare arms pins, wooden pricks, nails, sprigs of rosemary; and with this horrible object, from low farms, poor pelting villages, sheepcotes, and mills, sometime with lunatic bans, sometime with pray-

[107]

ers, enforce their charity; . . . poor Tom? whom the foul
fiend hath led through fire and through flame, through
ford and whirlpool, o'er bog and quagmire; that hath
laid knives under his pillow and halters in his pew, set
ratsbane by his porridge, made him proud of heart, to
ride on a bay trotting horse over four-inch'd bridges,
to curse his own shadow for a traitor. You must learn
to know such slanders of the age, or else you may be
marvellously mistook.

A Courtier

->>><<<-

CAME there a certain lord, neat and trimly dress'd, fresh
as a bridegroom; and his chin new reap'd show'd like
a stubble land at harvest home. He was perfumed like
a milliner, and 'twixt his finger and his thumb he held
a pouncet box, which ever and anon he gave his nose,
and took't away again; who therewith angry, when it
next came there, took it in snuff; and still he smil'd and
talk'd; and as the soldiers bore dead bodies by, he call'd
them untaught knaves, unmannerly, to bring a slovenly
unhandsome corse betwixt the wind and his nobility.
With many holiday and lady terms he questioned me.
. . . He made me mad to see him shine so brisk, and
smell so sweet, and talk so like a waiting gentlewoman
of guns and drums and wounds—God save the mark!—
And telling me the sovereign'st thing on earth was par-
maceti for an inward bruise; and that it was great pity,
so it was, this villanous saltpetre should be digg'd out
of the bowels of the harmless earth, which many a good
tall fellow had destroy'd so cowardly; and but for these
vile guns, he would himself have been a soldier.

This fellow pecks up wit as pigeons pease, and utters
it again when God doth please; a snapper-up of uncon-
sidered trifles. He is wit's peddlar, and retails his wares
at wakes and wassails, meetings, markets, fairs; and we

that sell by gross, the Lord doth know, have not the grace to grace it with such show. This gallant pins the wenches on his sleeve. Had he been Adam, he had tempted Eve. 'A can carve too, and lisp. Why, this is he that kiss'd his hand away in courtesy. This is the ape of form, Monsieur the Nice, that, when he plays at tables, chides the dice in honourable terms. Nay, he can sing a mean most meanly; and in ushering mend him who can. The ladies call him sweet. The stairs, as he treads on them kiss his feet. This is the flow'r that smiles on every one to show his teeth as white as whale's-bone; and consciences that will not die in debt pay him the due of 'honey-tongu'd Boyet.' . . . A refined traveller, . . . a man in all the world's new fashion planted, that hath a mint of phrases in his brain; one whom the music of his own vain tongue doth ravish like enchanting harmony; a man of complements, whom right and wrong have chose as umpire of their mutiny.

He did comply with his dug before he suck'd it. Thus has he, and many more of the same bevy that I know the drossy age dotes on, only got the tune of the time and outward habit of encounter—a kind of yesty collection, which carries them through and through the most fann'd and winnowed opinions; and do but blow them to their trial—the bubbles are out.

A Big Talker

→»>«←

HE SPEAKS an infinite deal of nothing, more than any
man in all Venice; he his special nothing ever pro-
logues. His reasons are as two grains of wheat hid in
two bushels of chaff. You shall seek all day ere you find
them; and when you have them, they are not worth
the search. A gentleman . . . that loves to hear himself
talk and will speak more in a minute than he will stand
to in a month. Talkers are no good doers.

Hear him debate of commonwealth affairs, you would
say it hath been all in all his study; list him discourse
of war, and you shall hear a fearful battle rend'red you
in music; turn him to any cause of policy, the Gordian
knot of it he will unloose, familiar as his garter; that,
when he speaks, the air, a charter'd libertine, is still,
and the mute wonder lurketh in men's ears to steal his
sweet and honey'd sentences; so that the art and prac-
tic part of life must be the mistress to this theoric; a
good traveller is something at the latter end of a dinner;
but one that lies three thirds and uses a known truth to
pass a thousand nothings with, saving in dialogue of
compliment, and talking of the Alps and Appenines,
the Pyrenean and the river Po—it draws toward supper
and conclusion so. Here's a large mouth indeed, that
spits forth death, and mountains, rocks and seas; talks

[111]

as familiarly of roaring lions as maids of thirteen do of puppy-dogs! . . . He speaks plain cannon-fire and smoke and bounce; he gives the bastinado with his tongue. Our ears are cudgell'd; not a word of his but buffets better than a fist. . . . I was never so bethumped with words. He . . . talks like a knell and his hum is a battery. He sits in his state, as a thing made for Alexander.

On Woman's Rights, Against and For

-»>×«-

A WOMAN mov'd is like a fountain troubled, muddy, ill-seeming, thick, bereft of beauty; and while it is so, none so dry or thirsty will deign to sip or touch one drop of it. Thy husband is thy lord, thy life, thy keeper, thy head, thy sovereign; one that cares for thee and for thy maintenance; commits his body to painful labour both by sea and land, to watch the night in storms, the day in cold, whilst thou li'st warm at home, secure and safe; and craves no other tribute at thy hands but love, fair looks and true obedience—too little payment for so great a debt. Such duty as the subject owes the prince, even such a woman oweth to her husband; and when she is froward, peevish, sullen, sour, and not obedient to his honest will, what is she but a foul contending rebel and a graceless traitor to her loving lord? Why, headstrong liberty is lash'd with woe. There's nothing situate under heaven's eye but hath his bound in earth, in sea, in sky. The beasts, the fishes, and the winged fowls are their males' subjects and at their controls. Men, more divine, the masters of all these, Lords of the wide world and wild wat'ry seas, indu'd with intellectual sense and souls, of more preeminence than fish and fowls, are masters to their females, and their lords.

But it is their husbands' faults if wives do fall. Say

[113]

that they slack their duties and pour our treasures into foreign laps; or else break out in peevish jealousies, throwing restraint upon us; or say they strike us, or scant our former having in despite—why, we have galls; and though we have some grace, yet have we some revenge. Let husbands know their wives have sense like them. They see, and smell, and have their palates both for sweet and sour, as husbands have. What is it that they do when they change us for others? Is it sport? ... And doth affection breed it? ... Is't frailty that thus errs? ... And have we not affections, desires for sport, and frailty, as men have? Then let them use us well: else let them know, the ills we do, their ills instruct us so.

Youth and Age

-->>|<<-

THE satirical rogue says . . . that old men have grey beards; that their faces are wrinkled; their eyes purging thick amber and plum-tree gum; and that they have a plentiful lack of wit, together with most weak hams. Old, cold, wither'd, and of intolerable entrails.

Do you set down your name in the scroll of youth, that are written down old with all the characters of age? Have you not a moist eye, a dry hand, a yellow cheek, a white beard, a decreasing leg, an increasing belly? Is not your voice broken, your wind short, your chin double, your wit single, and every part about you blasted with antiquity? And will you yet call yourself young? When the age is in, the wit is out.

A good leg will fall, a straight back will stoop, a black beard will turn white, a curl'd pate will grow bald, a fair face will wither, a full eye will wax hollow; but a good heart . . . is the sun and the moon; or rather, the sun, and not the moon, for it shines bright and never changes, but keeps his course truly. The elder I wax, the better I shall appear. My comfort is, that old age, that ill layer-up of beauty, can do no more spoil upon my face. Give me always a little, lean, old, chopp'd, bald shot. I would there were no age between ten and three-and-twenty, or that youth would sleep out the rest; for there is nothing in the between but getting wenches with child, wronging the ancientry, stealing, fighting. I had rather have skipp'd from sixteen years of age to sixty, to have turn'd my leaping time into a crutch.

This policy and reverence of age makes the world bitter to the rest of our times; keeps our fortunes from us till our oldness cannot relish them. I begin to find an idle and fond bondage in the oppression of aged tyranny, who sways, not as it hath power, but as it is suffer'd. . . . Sons at perfect age, and fathers declining, the father should be as ward to the son, and the son manage his revenue. The younger rises when the old doth fall.

Our own precedent passions do instruct us what levity's in youth. All's brave that youth mounts and folly guides. To be fantastic may become a youth, for youth no less becomes the light and careless livery that it wears than settled age his sables and his weeds, importing health and graveness. Lust and liberty creep in the minds and marrows of your youth, that 'gainst the stream of virtue they may strive and drown themselves in riot! Such wanton, wild, and usual slips as are companions noted and most known to youth and liberty, . . . as gaming, . . . or drinking, fencing, swearing, quarrelling, drabbing; in the morn and liquid dew of youth contagious blastments are most imminent. By heaven, it is as proper to our age to cast beyond ourselves in our opinions as it is common for the younger sort to lack discretion.

Crabbed age and youth cannot live together: youth is

[116]

full of pleasance, age is full of care; youth like summer
morn, age like winter weather; youth like summer
brave, . . . age's breath is short; youth is nimble, age
is lame; youth is hot and bold, age is weak, . . . youth
is wild, and age is tame. Age, I do abhor thee; youth I
do adore thee.

A Perfect Horse

→»)«←

LET my horse have his due. . . . It is the best horse of
Europe. . . . He bounds from the earth, as if his entrails
were hairs; *le cheval volant,* the Pegasus, *avec les na-
rines de feu!* When I bestride him, I soar, I am a hawk.
He trots the air. The earth sings when he touches it.
The basest horn of his hoof is more musical than the
pipe of Hermes. He's of the colour of the nutmeg. And
of the heat of the ginger. It is a beast for Perseus: he
is pure air and fire; and the dull elements of earth and
water never appear in him, but only in patient stillness
while his rider mounts him. He is indeed a horse, and
all other jades you may call beasts. . . .

It is a most absolute and excellent horse . . . the
prince of palfreys. His neigh is like the bidding of a
monarch, and his countenance enforces homage. . . . The
man hath no wit that cannot, from the rising of the
lark to the lodging of the lamb, vary deserved praise
on my palfrey. It is a theme as fluent as the sea. Turn
the sands into eloquent tongues, and my horse is argument for them all. 'Tis a subject for a sovereign to reason on, and for a sovereign's sovereign to ride on; and
for the world, familiar to us and unknown, to lay apart
their particular functions and wonder at him. I once

[118]

writ a sonnet in his praise and began thus, 'Wonder of nature!'

Imperiously he leaps, he neighs, he bounds, and now his woven girths he breaks asunder; the bearing earth with his hard hoof he wounds, whose hollow womb resounds like heaven's thunder; the iron bit he crusheth 'tween his teeth, controlling what he was controlled with. His ears up-prick'd; his braised hanging mane upon his compass'd crest . . . stand on end; his nostrils drink the air, and forth again, as from a furnace, vapours doth he send; his eye, which scornfully glisters like fire, shows his hot courage and his high desire. Sometimes he trots, as if he told the steps, with gentle majesty and modest pride; anon he rears upright, curvets and leaps, as who should say, 'Lo, thus my strength is tried, and this I do to captivate the eye of the fair breeder that is standing by.' What recketh he his rider's angry stir, his flattering 'Holla' or his 'Stand, I say'? What cares he now for curb or pricking spur? For rich caparisons or trappings gay? . . .

Look, when a painter would surpass the life in limning out a well-proportioned steed, his art with nature's workmanship at strife, as if the dead the living should exceed—so did this horse excel a common one in shape, in courage, colour, pace, and bone. Round-hoof'd, short-jointed, fetlocks shag and long, broad breast, full eye, small head, and nostril wide, high crest, short ears, straight legs and passing strong, thin mane, thick tail, broad buttock, tender hide: look, what a horse should have he did not lack, save a proud rider on so proud a back.

[119]

England

→⟫✕⟨←

WHEN Julius Caesar (whose remembrance yet lives in men's eyes and will to ears and tongues be theme and hearing ever) was in this Britain and conquer'd it, Cassibelan ... (famous in Caesar's praises, no whit less than in his feats deserving it) for him and his succession granted Rome a tribute, yearly three thousand pounds. ... There be many Caesars, ere such another Julius. ... A kind of conquest Caesar made here; but made not here his brag of 'came, and saw, and overcame.' With shame (the first that ever touch'd him) he was carried from off our coast, twice beaten; and his shipping, poor ignorant baubles, on our terrible seas, like eggshells mov'd upon their surges, crack'd as easily 'gainst our rocks; for joy whereof the fam'd Cassibelan, who was once at point ... to master Caesar's sword, made Lud's Town with rejoicing fires bright and Britons strut with courage. In our not-fearing Britain ... our countrymen are men more order'd than when Julius Caesar smil'd at their lack of skill but found their courage worthy his frowning at. Their discipline (now winged with their courages) will make known to their approvers they are people such that mend upon the world.

England breeds very valiant creatures. Their mastiffs

are of unmatchable courage. Foolish curs, that run winking into the mouth of a Russian bear and have their heads crush'd like rotten apples! You may as well say that's a valiant flea that dare eat his breakfast on the lip of a lion. . . . And the men do sympathize with the mastiffs in robustious and rough coming on, leaving their wits with their wives; and then give them great meals of beef and iron and steel, they will eat like wolves and fight like devils. Froissart . . . records England all Olivers and Rowlands bred during the time Edward the Third did reign. More truly now may this be verified; for none but Samsons and Goliases it sendeth forth to skirmish. One to ten? Lean raw-bon'd rascals—who would e'er suppose they had such courage and audacity?

I' th' world's volume our Britain seems as of it, but not in't; in a great pool a swan's nest. This royal throne of kings, this scept'red isle, this earth of majesty, this seat of Mars, this other Eden, demi-paradise, this fortress built by Nature for herself against infection and the hand of war, this happy breed of men, this little world, this precious stone set in the silver sea, which serves it in the office of a wall, or as a moat defensive to a house, against the envy of less happier lands; this blessed plot, this earth, this realm, this England, this nurse, this teeming womb of royal kings, fear'd by their breed and famous by their birth, renowned for their deeds as far from home, for Christian service and true chivalry, as is the sepulchre in stubborn Jewry of the world's ransom, blessed Mary's son; this land of such dear souls, this dear, dear land, dear for her reputation through the world. . . . England, bound in with the triumphant sea, whose rocky shore beats back the envious siege of wat'ry Neptune.

This England never did, nor never shall, lie at the proud foot of a conqueror but when it first did help to wound itself. Now these her princes are come home again, come the three corners of the world in arms, and we shall shock them. Naught shall make us rue if England to itself do rest but true. O England! model to thy inward greatness, like little body with a mighty heart, what mightst thou do that honour would thee do, were all thy children kind and natural!

Key

→»)«←

OF TRUTH

How this world is given ... :	*1 Henry IV*, v. 4. 149-150
Truth's a dog must to ... :	*King Lear*, i. 4. 124-126
There is scarce truth ... :	*Measure for Measure*, iii. 2. 240-242
What authority and show ... :	*Much Ado About Nothing*, iv. 1. 36-38
So may the outward shows ... :	*The Merchant of Venice*, iii. 2. 73-88
The devil can cite scripture ... :	*The Merchant of Venice*, i. 3. 99-103
And oftentimes, to win us ... :	*Macbeth*, i. 3. 123-126
If circumstances lead me ... :	*Hamlet*, ii. 2. 157-159
For truth can never be ... :	*Pericles*, v. 1. 203-204
Then this is all as true ... :	*Measure for Measure*, v. 1. 44-46
The truth should live from ... :	*Richard III*, iii. 1. 76-78
Who tells me true ... :	*Antony and Cleopatra*, i. 2. 102-103

OF TIME

Time travels in divers paces ... :	*As You Like It*, iii. 2. 326-351
Time hath ... a wallet at his ... :	*Troilus and Cressida*, iii. 3. 145-153
Let not virtue seek ... :	*Troilus and Cressida*, iii. 3. 169-170
What they do in present ... :	*Troilus and Cressida*, iii. 3. 163-169
One touch of nature makes ... :	*Troilus and Cressida*, iii. 3. 175-180
Have you not heard that ... :	*Comedy of Errors*, iv. 2. 59-60
Reckoning time ... :	*Sonnet CXV*, 5-8

Devouring time . . . :	*Sonnet* XIX, 1
Time that gave doth now . . . :	*Sonnet* LX, 8-12
Beauty, wit, high birth . . . :	*Troilus and Cressida,* iii. 111. 171-174
Do whate'er thou wilt . . . :	*Sonnet* XIX, 6-7
Do thy worst old time . . . :	*Sonnet* XIX, 13
Misshapen Time . . . :	*Rape of Lucrece,* 925
Sluttish Time . . . :	*Sonnet* LV, 4
Copesmate of ugly Night . . . :	*The Rape of Lucrece,* 925-933
Cancelled my fortunes . . . :	*The Rape of Lucrece,* 934-952
Time is the nurse and . . . :	*Two Gentlemen of Verona,* iii. 1. 243
Every time serves for . . . :	*Antony and Cleopatra,* ii. 2. 9-10
The baby finger of the . . . :	*Troilus and Cressida,* i. 3. 345-346
Time and the hour runs . . . :	*Macbeth,* i. 3. 147
Time shall unfold what . . . :	*King Lear,* i. 1. 283
Time's glory . . . :	*The Rape of Lucrece,* 939
To make the child a man . . . :	*The Rape of Lucrece,* 934
To calm contending kings . . . :	*The Rape of Lucrece,* 939
To fine the hate of foes . . . :	*The Rape of Lucrece,* 936-937
To unmask falsehood . . . :	*The Rape of Lucrece,* 940-943
Whereby I see that Time's . . . :	*Pericles,* ii. 3. 45-47
The end crowns all . . . :	*Troilus and Cressida,* iv. 5. 224-226

FLUX OR MUTABILITY

That one might read . . . :	*2 Henry IV,* iii. 1. 45-56
All that lives . . . :	*Hamlet,* i. 2. 73-74
We fat all creatures . . . :	*Hamlet,* iv. 3. 24-33
To what base uses . . . :	*Hamlet,* v. 1. 223-237
Great Princes' favorites . . . :	*Sonnet* XXV, 5-12
Like as the waves . . . :	*Sonnet* LX, 1-7
When I consider . . . :	*Sonnet* XV, 1-8
When I have seen . . . :	*Sonnet* LXIV, 1-12
What strong hand . . . :	*Sonnet* LXV, 11
The cloud-capp'd towers, . . . :	*The Tempest,* iv. 1. 152-155
This great world . . . :	*King Lear,* iv. 6. 137-138

OF LOVE

I do much wonder	*Much Ado About Nothing,* ii. 3. 9-14

I will not be sworn ... :   *Much Ado About Nothing,* ii. 3. 24-28

Love is a smoke rais'd ... :   *Romeo and Juliet,* i. 1. 197-201
As in the sweetest bud ... :   *Two Gentlemen of Verona,* i. 1. 42-48

Love is your master ... :   *Two Gentlemen of Verona,* i. 1. 39-41

Love is full of unbefitting ... :   *Love's Labour's Lost,* v. 2. 769-772
It is to be all ... :   *As You Like It,* v. 2. 100-104
There lives within the ... :   *Hamlet,* iv. 7. 115-119
Men have died from time ... :   *As You Like It,* iv. 1. 106-108
Things base and vile ... :   *A Midsummer Night's Dream,* i. 1. 232-234

Other slow arts entirely ... :   *Love's Labour's Lost,* iv. 3. 334-349

Let me not to the ... :   *Sonnet* CXVI, 1-14

OF LUST

If the balance of our ... :   *Othello,* i. 3. 330-340
Th' expense of spirit ... :   *Sonnet* CXXIX
You cannot call it love ... :   *Hamlet,* iii. 4. 68-76
Virtue as it never will ... :   *Hamlet,* i. 5. 53-57
Rebellious hell, if thou ... :   *Hamlet,* iii. 4. 82-88
Call it not love ... :   *Venus and Adonis,* 792-804

MARRIAGE AND SINGLE LIFE

Tell me why ... :   *All's Well That Ends Well,* i. 3. 29-32

We must be married ... :   *As You Like It,* iii. 3. 99
Will you be married? ... :   *As You Like It,* iii. 3. 79-83
Get you to church ... :   *As You Like It,* iii. 3. 86-87
By marriage all ... :   *Antony and Cleopatra,* ii. 2. 133-136

Marriage is a matter ... :   *1 Henry VI,* v. 5. 55-65
O curse of marriage ... :   *Othello,* iii. 3. 268-275
I will rather trust ... :   *The Merry Wives of Windsor,* ii. 2. 316-323

The fittest time ... :   *Coriolanus,* iv. 3. 33-35
As horns are odious ... :   *As You Like It,* iii. 3. 52-58

Horns which such . . . :	*As You Like It*, iv. 1. 59-60
What shall he have . . . :	*As You Like It*, iv. 2. 11-19
He may sleep . . . :	*2 Henry IV*, i. 2. 50-53
Get thee a wife . . . :	*Much Ado About Nothing*, v. 4. 124-126
Should all despair . . . :	*The Winter's Tale*, i. 2. 198-200
There have been . . . :	*The Winter's Tale*, i. 2. 190-196
He that ears my . . . :	*All's Well That Ends Well*, i. 3. 48-54
A young man . . . :	*All's Well That Ends Well*, ii. 3. 315
She's not well married . . . :	*Romeo and Juliet*, iv. 5. 77-78
If thou wilt . . . :	*Hamlet*, iii. 1. 144-146
I knew a wench . . . :	*The Taming of the Shrew*, iv. 4. 99-101
I have railed . . . :	*Much Ado About Nothing*, ii. 3. 246-247
In brief, since . . . :	*Much Ado About Nothing*, v. 4. 106-109
But let still . . . :	*Twelfth Night*, ii. 4. 30-36
Earthlier happy is . . . :	*A Midsummer Night's Dream*, i. 1. 76-78
Wives may be merry . . . :	*The Merry Wives of Windsor*, iv. 2. 107
I take today . . . :	*Troilus and Cressida*, ii. 2. 61
whose beauty did . . . :	*All's Well That Ends Well*, v. 3. 16-18
That man i' th' world . . . :	*Henry VIII*, ii. 4. 132-139
Ye gods, render me . . . :	*Julius Caesar*, ii. 1. 303-304

OF AMBITION

I hold ambition . . . :	*Hamlet*, ii. 2. 267-269
A circle in the . . . :	*1 Henry VI*, i. 2. 133-135
Dreams indeed are . . . :	*Hamlet*, ii. 2. 263-265
Ambition, the . . . :	*Antony and Cleopatra*, iii. 1. 22-24
Seeking the bubble . . . :	*As You Like It*, ii. 7. 152-153
Makes mouths at the . . . :	*Hamlet*, iv. 4. 50-54
Man and birds . . . :	*2 Henry VI*, ii. 1. 8
Lowliness is young . . . :	*Julius Caesar*, ii. 1. 22-27

[126]

And out of question...:	*Love's Labour's Lost,* iv. 1. 30-33
Th' abuse of...:	*Julius Caesar,* ii. 1. 17-18
Virtue is chok'd...:	*2 Henry VI,* iii. 1. 143
O! the fierce...:	*Timon of Athens,* iv. 2. 30
Vautling ambition...:	*Macbeth,* i. 7. 27
Thriftless ambition...:	*Macbeth,* ii. 4. 28
Which swell'd so...:	*Cymbeline,* iii. 1. 50
Fling away ambition...:	*Henry VIII,* iii. 2. 440-442
Vain pomp and...:	*Henry VIII,* iii. 2. 365-372
Better to be...:	*Henry VIII,* ii. 3. 19-22

FORTUNE

Fortune is painted blind...:	*Henry V,* iii. 6. 33-40
I have upon a high...:	*Timon of Athens,* i. 1. 63-92
Let us sit and mock...:	*As You Like It,* i. 2. 34-48
Will Fortune never come...:	*2 Henry IV,* iv. 3. 104-107
Out, out, thou strumpet...:	*Hamlet,* ii. 2. 515-518
Wisdom and fortune combating...:	*Antony and Cleopatra,* iii. 13. 79-81
Fortune brings in some boats...:	*Cymbeline,* iv. 3. 46
Our indiscretion sometime...:	*Hamlet,* v. 2. 8-11
I know not what counts...:	*Antony and Cleopatra,* ii. 6. 54-57

OF SLEEP

Thy best of rest is...:	*Measure for Measure,* iii. 1. 17
Sleep, that sometimes...:	*A Midsummer Night's Dream,* iii. 2. 435
The golden dew of...:	*Richard III,* iv. 1. 84
The innocent sleep...:	*Macbeth,* ii. 2. 36-39
These should be hours...:	*Henry VIII,* v. 1. 2-5
Weary with toil, I haste...:	*Sonnet XXVII,* 1-8
O sleep, O gentle sleep...:	*2 Henry IV,* iii. 1. 5-30
'Tis not the balm...:	*Henry V,* iv. 1. 277-298

OF FRIENDSHIP

I count myself...:	*Richard II,* ii. 3. 46-49
What need we have...:	*Timon of Athens,* i. 2. 98-107
Thou dost conspire...:	*Othello,* iii. 3. 142-143
The amity that...:	*Troilus and Cressida,* ii. 3. 110-111

Friends now fast sworn . . . :	*Coriolanus,* iv. 4. 12-22
The great man down . . . :	*Hamlet,* iii. 2. 218-219
Those friends thou . . . :	*Hamlet,* i. 3. 62-65
Hollow men . . . :	*Julius Caesar,* iv. 2. 23-27
Where you are . . . :	*Henry VIII,* ii. 1. 126-131
He that wants . . . :	*As You Like It,* iii. 2. 24-26

DRINKING—AGAINST

O thou invisible . . . :	*Othello,* ii. 3. 282-284
God, that men . . . :	*Othello,* ii. 3. 291-294
Every inordinate . . . :	*Othello,* ii. 3. 311-312
It's monstrous . . . :	*Antony and Cleopatra,* ii. 7. 105
Drunk? and speak . . . :	*Othello,* ii. 3. 280-283
Ingrateful man . . . :	*Timon of Athens,* iv. 3. 194-195
I learn'd it in . . . :	*Othello,* ii. 3. 78-86
Though I am . . . :	*Hamlet,* i. 4. 14-22

DRINKING—FOR

Come, come, good . . . :	*Othello,* ii. 3. 313-315
Dost thou think . . . :	*Twelfth Night,* ii. 3. 124-125
There's never none . . . :	*2 Henry IV,* iv. 3. 97-135

OF IGNORANCE AND LEARNING

There is no . . . :	*Twelfth Night,* iv. 2. 46
Gross and miserable . . . :	*2 Henry VI,* iv. 2. 178
Thou monster . . . :	*Love's Labour's Lost,* iv. 2. 24
The common curse . . . :	*Trolius and Cressida,* ii. 3. 30
How deformed . . . :	*Love's Labour's Lost,* iv. 2. 23
Dull, unfeeling . . . :	*Richard II,* i. 3. 168
Thou praisest . . . :	*Othello,* ii. 1. 144
Ignorant . . . :	*Othello,* v. 2. 164
An idiot holds . . . :	*Titus Andronicus,* v. 1. 79
We, ignorant of . . . :	*Antony and Cleopatra,* ii. 1. 5-6
What a thrice . . . :	*The Tempest,* v. 1. 295-297
Ignorance is the . . . :	*2 Henry VI,* iv. 7. 78-79
O this learning . . . :	*The Taming of the Shrew,* i. 2. 160
And though I . . . :	*Love's Labour's Lost,* i. 1. 112-113
I held it ever . . . :	*Pericles,* iii. 2. 26-31
Fitter is my . . . :	*1 Henry VI,* v. 1. 22

What is the end ...:   *Love's Labour's Lost*, i. 1. 55-58
If study's ...:   *Love's Labour's Lost*, i. 1. 67
Study is like ...:   *Love's Labour's Lost*, i. 1. 83-85
Universal plodding ...:   *Love's Labour's Lost*, iv. 3. 305-306
Small have ...:   *Love's Labour's Lost*, i. 1. 86-87
So study evermore ...:   *Love's Labour's Lost*, i. 1. 143-147
All delights are ...:   *Love's Labour's Lost*, i. 1. 72-79
These earthly ...:   *Love's Labour's Lost*, i. 1. 87-91
None are so ...:   *Love's Labour's Lost*, v. 2. 69-72
O knowledge ...:   *As You Like It*, iii. 3. 10-11
In brief ... study ...:   *The Taming of the Shrew*, i. 1. 40
Our bodies are ...:   *Othello*, i. 3. 323-324
The even mead ...:   *Henry V*, v. 2. 48-58

OF PHILOSOPHY

We have our philosophical ...:   *All's Well That Ends Well*, ii. 3. 2-4
Hang up philosophy ...:   *Romeo and Juliet*, iii. 3. 57-60
Who can hold a fire ...:   *Richard II*, i. 3. 294-301
For there was never yet ...:   *Much Ado About Nothing*, v. 1. 35-38
A wretched soul bruis'd ...:   *Comedy of Errors*, ii. 1. 34-37
Brother, men can counsel ...:   *Much Ado About Nothing*, v. 1. 20-31
It is a good divine ...:   *The Merchant of Venice*, i. 2. 15-19
These deeds must not ...:   *Macbeth*, ii. 2. 33-34
sicklied o'er ...:   *Hamlet*, iii. 1. 85
You do unbend ...:   *Macbeth*, ii. 2. 45-46
Of your philosophy you ...:   *Julius Caesar*, iv. 3. 145-146
To be generous, guiltless ...:   *Twelfth Night*, i. 5. 98-101
There's nothing either good ...: *Hamlet*, ii. 2. 255-257
All places that the eye ...:   *Richard II*, i. 3. 275-276

OF THE VIRTUE OF LAUGHTER

Let us say ...:   *The Merchant of Venice*, i. 1. 47-56
You have too much ...:   *The Merchant of Venice*, i. 1. 74-82
A merry heart ...:   *2 Henry IV*, v. 3. 50

[129]

A merry heart goes...:   *The Winter's Tale,* iv. 3. 134-135
Why should a man...:   *The Merchant of Venice,* i. 1. 83-99
Seeing too much...:   *The Taming of the Shrew,* induc-
                           tion. ii. 134-138

OF MENTAL PAIN

Better be with...:   *Macbeth,* iii. 2. 19-22
Better I were...:   *King Lear,* iv. 6. 288-289
But I am bound...:   *King Lear,* iv. 7. 46
Canst thou...:   *Macbeth,* v. 3. 40-44
Not poppy nor...:   *Othello,* iii. 3. 330-331
Some griefs...:   *Cymbeline,* iii. 2. 33
We are not...:   *King Lear,* ii. 4. 108-110
Each substance...:   *Richard II,* ii. 2. 14
Grief would...:   *All's Well That Ends Well,* iii. 4.
                           42

Give sorrow words...:   *Macbeth,* iv. 3. 209-210
Sorrow concealed...:   *Titus Andronicus,* ii. 4. 36-37
Deep sounds make...:   *The Rape of Lucrece,* 1329-1330
Sorrow breaks...:   *Richard III,* i. 4. 76-77
Grief dallied...:   *The Rape of Lucrece,* 1120
When sorrows come...:   *Hamlet,* iv. 5. 78-79
One sorrow never...:   *Pericles,* i. 4. 63-64
For sorrow, like...:   *The Rape of Lucrece,* 1493-1494
Oft have I heard...:   *2 Henry VI,* iv. 4. 1-2
Moderate lamentation...:   *All's Well That Ends Well,* i. 1.
                           64-67

But to persever...:   *Hamlet,* i. 2. 92-97
What's gone and...:   *The Winter's Tale,* iii. 2. 223-224
Things without all...:   *Macbeth,* iii. 2. 11-12
He robs himself...:   *Othello,* i. 3. 209
Gnarling sorrow...:   *Richard II,* i. 3. 292-293
In poison there...:   *2 Henry IV,* i. 1. 137-145
To be worst...:   *King Lear,* iv. 1. 2-6

OF THE FORCE OF THE IMAGINATION

I talk of dreams...:   *Romeo and Juliet,* i. 4. 97-103
You laugh...:   *Antony and Cleopatra,* v. 2. 74

The best in this....:	*A Midsummer Night's Dream,* v. 1. 213-215
Such tricks hath...:	*A Midsummer Night's Dream,* v. 1. 18-22
Lovers and madmen...:	*A Midsummer Night's Dream,* v. 1. 4-11
There may be in the cup...:	*The Winter's Tale,* ii. 1. 39-45
The sense of death...:	*Measure for Measure,* iii. 1. 78-81
Fools...in th'...:	*The Lover's Complaint,* 136-140
Present fears are less...:	*Macbeth,* i. 3. 135-136
I yield to that suggestion...:	*Macbeth,* i. 3. 134-142
I could be bounded...:	*Hamlet,* ii. 2. 260-262

ON LIFE

Life is a shuttle...:	*The Merry Wives of Windsor,* v. 1. 25
The web of our life...:	*All's Well That Ends Well,* iv. 3. 83-84
The single and peculiar...:	*Hamlet,* iii. 3. 11-13
with...incident...:	*Timon of Athens,* v. 1. 203-204
How brief the life...:	*As You Like It,* iii. 2. 137-138
A man's life's...:	*Hamlet,* v. 2. 74
It is silliness...:	*Othello,* i. 3. 309
that life is better...:	*Measure for Measure,* v. 1. 402-403
My life I never...:	*King Lear,* i. 1. 157
there's nothing serious...:	*Macbeth,* ii. 3. 98-101
as flies to wanton boys...:	*King Lear,* iv. 1. 36
When we are born...:	*King Lear,* iv. 6, 186-187
we came crying...:	*King Lear,* iv. 6. 182-184
men must endure...:	*King Lear,* v. 2. 9-11
'Tis but an hour...:	*As You Like It,* ii. 7. 24-28
This is the state...:	*Henry VIII,* iii. 2. 352-358
Life's but a walking shadow...:	*Macbeth,* v. 5. 24-28
The weariest and...:	*Measure for Measure,* iii. 1. 129-132
Let me live...:	*All's Well That Ends Well,* iv. 3. 273-274
Simply the thing...:	*All's Well That Ends Well,* iv. 3. 369-370

[131]

ADVERSITY

To wilful men...:	*King Lear*, ii. 4. 305
The art of our...:	*King Lear*, iii. 2. 70-71
Nothing almost...:	*King Lear*, ii. 2. 172-173
You were us'd...:	*Coriolanus*, iv. 1. 3-7
The sea being...:	*Troilus and Cressida*, i. 3. 34-45
In the reproof...:	*Troilus and Cressida*, i. 3. 33-34
I'll give thee...:	*Romeo and Juliet*, iii. 3. 54-55
What thy soul...:	*Richard II*, i. 3. 286-291
They are as sick...:	*The Merchant of Venice*, i. 2. 6-10
Our basest beggars...:	*King Lear*, ii. 4. 268-273
Checks and disasters...:	*Troilus and Cressida*, i. 3. 5-9
There is some...:	*Henry V*, iv. 1. 4-13
'Tis good for...:	*Henry V*, iv. 1. 18-23
The worst is not...:	*King Lear*, iv. 1. 27

OF DEATH

Reason thus with life...:	*Measure for Measure*, iii. 1. 6-39
To sue to live...:	*Measure for Measure*, iii. 1. 42-43
if it be now...:	*Hamlet*, v. 2. 231-234
Cowards die...:	*Julius Caesar*, ii. 2. 32-37
Within the hollow crown...:	*Richard II*, iii. 2. 160-170
Fear no more...:	*Cymbeline*, iv. 2. 258-269

SUICIDE, AGAINST AND FOR

Against self-slaughter...:	*Cymbeline*, iii. 4. 78
O, our lives' sweetness...:	*King Lear*, v. 3. 184
I know not how,...:	*Julius Caesar*, v. 1. 102-107
O...that the Everlasting...:	*Hamlet*, i, 2. 132
Is wretchedness deprived...:	*King Lear*, iv. 6. 61-64
Therein ye Gods...:	*Julius Caesar*, i. 3. 91-100
Our dungy earth...:	*Antony and Cleopatra*, i. 1. 35
And it is great...:	*Antony and Cleopatra*, v. 2. 4-8

OF RICHES

How quickly nature falls...:	*2 Henry IV*, iv. 5. 66-80
'Tis gold which buys...:	*Cymbeline*, ii. 3. 72-75
'Tis certain greatness...:	*Troilus and Cressida*, iii. 3. 75-87

Gold! Yellow, glittering ... :	*Timon of Athens*, iv. 3. 26-41
O thou sweet king-killer ... :	*Timon of Athens*, iv. 3. 382-390

ON CEREMONY

What infinite ... :	*Henry V.* iv. 1. 253-268
Ceremony was but ... :	*Timon of Athens*, i. 2. 15-17
Be sick, great ... :	*Henry V*, iv. 1. 268-274
Behold how pomp ... :	*Antony and Cleopatra*, v. 2. 150
What need these ... :	*Timon of Athens*, i. 2. 248-249
To be possess'd ... :	*King John*, iv. 2. 9-16
Vain pomp and ... :	*Henry VIII*, iii. 2. 365
Let the candied ... :	*Hamlet*, iii. 2. 65
What is pomp, rule ... :	*3 Henry VI*, v. 4. 27
O the fierce ... :	*Timon of Athens*, iv. 2. 30
Willing misery ... :	*Timon of Athens*, iv. 3. 242-247
I am for the house ... :	*All's Well That Ends Well*, iv. 5. 53-58
The primrose way ... :	*Macbeth*, ii. 3. 21

OF MOBS

What would you have ... :	*Coriolanus*, i. 1. 172-188
They'll sit by the fire ... :	*Coriolanus*, i. 1. 195-199
It hath been taught ... :	*Antony and Cleopatra*, i. 4. 41-47
An habitation giddy ... :	*2 Henry IV*, i. 3. 89-100
Was ever feather ... :	*2 Henry VI*, iv. 9. 57-58

ON THE INJUSTICE OF SOCIETY

O that estates ... :	*The Merchant of Venice*, ii. 9. 41-49
A man may see ... :	*King Lear*, iv. 6. 153-171
The jury, passing ... :	*Measure for Measure*, ii. 1. 18-23
The blind mole ... :	*Pericles*, i. 1. 100-102
Raise me this ... :	*Timon of Athens*, iv. 3. 9-13
Tir'd with all ... :	*Sonnet LVI*, 1-13

RETRIBUTIVE JUSTICE

Justice always ... :	*Love's Labour's Lost*, iv. 3. 384
In the corrupted ... :	*Hamlet*, iii. 3. 57-61

[133]

There sits a judge...:	*Henry VIII,* iii. 1. 100
There the action...:	*Hamlet,* iii. 3. 61-64
He that steeps...:	*King John,* iii. 4. 147-148
If th' assassination...:	*Macbeth,* i. 7. 2-12
The gods are just...:	*King Lear,* v. 3. 170-171
He that of greatest...:	*All's Well That Ends Well,* ii. 1. 139-140
Foul deeds will...:	*Hamlet,* i. 2. 257-258
For murther, though...:	*Hamlet,* ii. 2. 622-623
Know'st thou not...:	*Richard II,* iii. 2. 36-46
Tremble, thou wretch...:	*King Lear,* iii. 2. 51-57
Beyond the infinite...:	*King John,* iv. 3. 117-119
Close pent-up...:	*King Lear,* iii. 2. 57-59
If that the heavens...:	*King Lear,* iv. 2. 46-50

OF RESPONSIBILITY FOR CRIME

These late eclipses...:	*King Lear,* i. 2. 112-119
Unnaturalness between...:	*King Lear,* i. 2. 157-163
We have seen...:	*King Lear,* i. 2. 122-124
This is the...:	*King Lear,* i. 2. 129-145
'Tis in ourselves...:	*Othello,* i. 3. 322-332
Our remedies oft...:	*All's Well That Ends Well,* i. 1. 231-241
The fault...is not...:	*Julius Caesar,* i. 2. 140-141

OF HONOUR

Honours thrive...:	*All's Well That Ends Well,* ii. 3. 142-148
From lowest place...:	*All's Well That Ends Well,* ii. 3. 132-138
'Tis the mind...:	*Taming of the Shrew,* iv. 3. 174-176
If you were...:	*Pericles,* iv. 6. 99-101
The time of life...:	*1 Henry IV,* v. 2. 82-84
Can honour set...:	*1 Henry IV,* v. 1. 133-142
The fewer men...:	*Henry V,* iv. 3. 22
Honour travels...:	*Troilus and Cressida,* iii. 3. 154-164
By heaven, methinks...:	*1 Henry IV,* i. 3. 201-205
Set honour in...:	*Julius Caesar,* i. 2. 86-89

| If it be a sin . . . : | *Henry V*, iv. 3. 28-29 |
| Mine honour is . . . : | *Richard II*, i. 1. 182-183 |

ON BEAUTY

The ornament of beauty . . . :	*Sonnet LXX*, 3
Nature with a beauteous . . . :	*Twelfth Night*, i. 2. 48-49
Look on beauty . . . :	*The Merchant of Venice*, iii. 2. 88-96
The power of beauty . . . :	*Hamlet*, iii. 1. 111-115
Beauty is but a vain . . . :	*The Passionate Pilgrim*, xiii. 1-11
Beauty too rich for use . . . :	*Romeo and Juliet*, i. 5. 49
Since brass, nor stone . . . :	*Sonnet LXV*, 1-8
When forty winters shall . . . :	*Sonnet II*, 1-4
Beauty's crest becomes . . . :	*Love's Labour's Lost*, iv. 3. 256
When would you have found . . . :	*Love's Labour's Lost*, iv. 3. 299-331
From women's eyes . . . :	*Love's Labour's Lost*, iv. 3. 350-353
From fairest creatures . . . :	*Sonnet I*, 1-2

OF MUSIC

Know the cause . . . :	*The Taming of the Shrew*, iii. 1. 10-12
Music oft hath . . . :	*Measure for Measure*, iv. 1. 14-15
Do but note . . . :	*The Merchant of Venice*, v. 1. 71-80
for Orpheus' lute . . . :	*Two Gentlemen of Verona*, iii. 2. 78-81
naught so stockish, . . . :	*The Merchant of Venice*, v. 1. 81-88
How sour sweet music is . . . :	*Richard II*, v. 5. 42-43
Soft stillness . . . :	*The Merchant of Venice*, v. 1. 56-65
So it is . . . :	*Richard II*, v. 5. 44
The tongues of dying men . . . :	*Richard II*, ii. 1. 5-14

POETRY

I do not know . . . :	*As You Like It*, iii. 3. 17-18
These fellows of . . . :	*Henry V*, v. 2. 163-166
The truest poetry . . . :	*As You Like It*, iii. 3. 19-22

When the blood . . . :	*Hamlet*, i. 3. 116-117
At lovers' . . . :	*Romeo and Juliet*, ii. 2. 92-93
What! A speaker . . . :	*Henry V*, v. 2. 166-167
I had rather . . . :	*1 Henry IV*, iii. 1. 129-135
Our poesy is a . . . :	*Timon of Athens*, i. 1. 20-25
It flies an eagle's flight . . . :	*Timon of Athens*, i. 1. 49-50
Much is the force . . . :	*Two Gentlemen of Verona*, iii. 2. 72
The poet's eye . . . :	*A Midsummer Night's Dream*, v. 1. 12-17
Never durst poet . . . :	*Love's Labour's Lost*, iv. 3. 346-349
Who will believe . . . :	*Sonnet XVII*, 1-8
When in the . . . :	*Sonnet CVI*, 1-12
But you shall . . . :	*Sonnet LV*, 3-4
When time is old . . . :	*Troilus and Cressida*, iii. 2. 192-196
When wastful war . . . :	*Sonnet LV*, 5-12
Not marble nor . . . :	*Sonnet LV*, 1-2

REPUTATION AND SLANDER

The purest treasure . . . :	*Richard II*, i. 1. 177-179
Good name in man . . . :	*Othello*, iii. 3. 155-161
Be thou as chaste . . . :	*Hamlet*, iii. 1. 140-142
Virtue itself . . . :	*Hamlet*, i. 3. 38
For calumny . . . :	*The Winter's Tale*, ii. 1. 73-74
No might nor . . . :	*Measure for Measure*, iii. 2. 196-199
'Tis slander, whose . . . :	*Cymbeline*, iii. 4. 35-39
Slander whose . . . :	*Hamlet*, iv. 1. 40-43
Kings, queens, and . . . :	*Cymbeline*, iii. 4. 39-41
For slander lives . . . :	*The Comedy of Errors*, iii. 1. 105-106
Rumor is a pipe . . . :	*2 Henry IV*, induction. 16-20

ON OPPORTUNITY

Who seeks, and . . . :	*Antony and Cleopatra*, ii. 7. 89-90
There is a tide . . . :	*Julius Caesar*, iv. 3. 218-224
Embrace we then . . . :	*1 Henry VI*, ii. 1. 13
If once it is . . . :	*1 Henry VI*, v. 4. 157-158

[136]

| Let's take the . . . : | *All's Well That Ends Well*, v. 3. 39-42 |
| O opportunity, thy . . . : | *The Rape of Lucrece*, 876-924 |

OF THE VIRTUE OF ACTION

Man—how dearly . . . :	*Troilus and Cressida*, iii. 3. 97-102
There is a kind . . . :	*Measure for Measure*, i. 1. 29-40
This is not . . . :	*Troilus and Cressida*, iii. 3. 102-123

OF INGRATITUDE

See the . . . :	*Timon of Athens*, iii. 2. 79-80
I hate ingratitude . . . :	*Twelfth Night*, iii. 4. 389-391
Old fellows . . . :	*Timon of Athens*, ii. 2. 223-228
Ingratitude is . . . :	*Coriolanus*, ii. 3. 10
Ingratitude, thou . . . :	*King Lear*, i. 4. 281-283
Sharper than a . . . :	*King Lear*, i. 4. 310-311
Filial ingratitude . . . :	*King Lear*, iii. 4. 14-16
Common mother . . . :	*Timon of Athens*, iv. 3. 177-192
Blow, winds, and . . . :	*King Lear*, iii. 2. 1-9

OF POLITICS AND POLITICIANS

Policy sits . . . :	*Timon of Athens*, iii. 2. 94
Conscience is a word . . . :	*Richard III*, v. 3. 310-311
I'll not meddle . . . :	*Richard III*, i. 4. 137-148
They tax our policy . . . :	*Troilus and Cressida*, i. 3. 197-210
The providence that's in . . . :	*Troilus and Cressida*, iii. 3. 196-204
Plague of your policy . . . :	*Henry VIII*, iii. 2. 259
Policy I hate, . . . :	*Twelfth Night*, iii. 2. 33
that same purpose-changer . . . :	*King John*, ii. 1. 567-580
The devil knew not what . . . :	*Timon of Athens*, iii. 3. 28-31
There's no art . . . :	*Macbeth*, i. 4. 11-12
When my outward . . . :	*Othello*, i. 1. 61-65
I seem a saint . . . :	*Richard III*, i. 3. 338
Look like the innocent . . . :	*Macbeth*, i. 5. 66-67
I'll drown more . . . :	*3 Henry VI*, iii. 2. 186-190
'Tis the sport to have . . . :	*Hamlet*, iii. 4. 206-207
I can add colours . . . :	*3 Henry VI*, iii. 2. 191-193

[137]

Nor sleep nor . . . :	*Coriolanus*, i. 10. 19-24
Tut, I have done . . . :	*Titus Andronicus*, v. 1. 141-144
Yet, to avoid deceit . . . :	*King John*, i. 1. 215-216
Am I politic . . . :	*The Merry Wives of Windsor*, iii. 1. 104-105

OF WAR

Shall we at last . . . :	*2 Henry VI*, v. 4. 107
Peace is nothing . . . :	*Coriolanus*, iv. 5. 234-246
And quietness grown . . . :	*Antony and Cleopatra*, i. 3. 52-53
Plenty and peace . . . :	*Cymbeline*, iii. 6. 21
I, in this weak . . . :	*Richard III*, i. 1. 24-25
Therefore . . . busy . . . :	*2 Henry IV*, iv. 5. 214
In peace there's . . . :	*Henry V*, iii. 1. 3-25
The gates of . . . :	*Henry V*, iii. 3. 10-27
World, thou hast . . . :	*Antony and Cleopatra*, iii. 5. 14-16
Now for the bare- . . . :	*King John*, iv. 3. 148-150
Now doth Death . . . :	*King John*, ii. 1. 352-354
Whose powers are . . . :	*Hamlet*, iv. 4. 9-26
Look . . . on fertile . . . :	*1 Henry VI*, iii. 3. 44-46
Now do I prophesy . . . :	*Julius Caesar*, iii. 1. 259-275

OF PEACE

Wherefore do you . . . :	*2 Henry IV*, iv. 1. 47-52
Thy threat'ning . . . :	*King John*, v. 2. 73-76
A peace is of . . . :	*2 Henry IV*, iv. 2. 89
Peace, dear nurse . . . :	*Henry V*, v. 2. 34
Enrich the time . . . :	*Richard III*, v. 5. 33-34
Piety and fear . . . :	*Timon of Athens*, iv. 1. 15-18
And sing the . . . :	*Henry VIII*, v. 5. 36
Our tradesmen . . . :	*Coriolanus*, iv. 6. 8-9
Peace shall still . . . :	*Hamlet*, v. 2. 41
The time of . . . :	*Antony and Cleopatra*, iv. 6. 5-7
Peace itself should . . . :	*Henry V*, ii. 4. 16-19

OF NATURE

In nature's infinite . . . :	*Antony and Cleopatra*, i. 2. 9-10
And I can speak . . . :	*Pericles*, iii. 2. 37-42
By turning over . . . :	*Pericles*, iii. 2. 33-36

[138]

many for many...:	*Romeo and Juliet*, ii. 3. 13-16
Diseased nature...:	*1 Henry IV*, iii. 1, 27-33
Death may usurp...:	*Pericles*, iii. 2. 82-86
Nature's above art...:	*King Lear*, iv. 6. 86
whose end, both...:	*Hamlet*, iii. 2. 25-27
labouring art can...:	*All's Well That Ends Well*, ii. 1. 121-122
To gild refined...:	*King John*, iv. 2. 11-16
I have heard...:	*The Winter's Tale*, iv. 4. 87-97
It is the show...:	*All's Well That Ends Well*, i. 3. 138-139
Nature is fine...:	*Hamlet*, iv. 5. 161-163
Base men being...:	*Othello*, ii. 1. 218-220
If nature...:	*Sonnet CXXVI*, 5-12
When Nature calls...:	*Sonnet IV*, 11-12
Nature never lends...:	*Measure for Measure*, i. 1. 38-41
Thou, Nature, art...:	*King Lear*, i. 2. 1-2

ON THE FORCE OF CUSTOM

Nature her custom holds...:	*Hamlet*, iv. 7. 188
What custom wills...:	*Coriolanus*, ii. 3. 124
We must not make...:	*Measure for Measure*, ii. 1. 1-4
New customs though they...:	*Henry VIII*, i. 3. 3
That monster, custom...:	*Hamlet*, iii. 4. 161-170

BACK TO NATURE

When Jove will...:	*Timon of Athens*, iv. 3. 108-110
Unfrequented woods...:	*Two Gentlemen of Verona*, v. 4. 2-3
Cities that of...:	*Pericles*, i. 4. 52-54
Did you but know...:	*Cymbeline*, iii. 3. 45-53
To the woods...:	*Timon of Athens*, iv. 1. 35-36
Are not...woods more...:	*As You Like It*, ii. 1. 3-17
Plenty and peace...:	*Cymbeline*, iii. 6. 21-22
Weariness can snore...:	*Cymbeline*, iii. 6. 33-35
Let the superfluous...:	*King Lear*, iv. 1. 68-72
Why should you...:	*Timon of Athens*, iv. 3. 420-424
Had I plantation...:	*The Tempest*, ii. 1. 142-168

ON THE NATURE OF MAN

O the difference ... :	*King Lear*, iv. 2. 26
All men are not ... :	*Cymbeline*, ii. 2. 4-5
In the catalogue ye ... :	*Macbeth*, iii. 1. 92-101
In the reproof of ... :	*Troilus and Cressida*, i. 3. 33-34
the protractive trials ... :	*Troilus and Cressida*, i. 3. 20-30
Will you tell me ... :	*2 Henry IV*, iii. 2. 275-278
Is not birth ... :	*Troilus and Cressida*, i. 2. 274-279
What a piece of work ... :	*Hamlet*, ii. 2. 315-321
We must think men ... :	*Othello*, iii. 4. 148
A noble nature may ... :	*Timon of Athens*, ii. 2. 218
Correction and instruction ... :	*Measure for Measure*, iii. 2. 33-34
In men, as in a rough-grown ... :	*The Rape of Lucrece*, 1249-1250
Virtue cannot so inoculate ... :	*Hamlet*, iii. 1. 119-120
We profess ourselves ... :	*The Winter's Tale*, iv. 4. 550-552
Were man but constant ... :	*Two Gentlemen of Verona*, v. 4. 110-112
Our natures do pursue ... :	*Measure for Measure*, i. 2. 132-134
I wonder men dare ... :	*Timon of Athens*, i. 2. 44
Thou almost mak'st me ... :	*The Merchant of Venice*, iv. 1. 130-131
There's nothing level ... :	*Timon of Athens*, iv. 3. 19
What! are men mad? ... :	*Cymbeline*, i. 6. 32-38

OF THE BEAST IN MAN

What is a man ... :	*Hamlet*, iv. 5. 34-39
Divided from fair ... :	*Hamlet*, iv. 5. 85
fox in stealth ... :	*King Lear*, iii. 4. 96
You may as well ... :	*The Merchant of Venice*, iv. 1. 71-80
Man, proud man ... :	*Measure for Measure*, ii. 2. 117-122
Wouldst thou have ... :	*Timon of Athens*, iv. 3. 325-352

OF A PERFECT MAN

He was a man ... :	*Hamlet*, i. 2. 187-188
the courtier's ... :	*Hamlet*, iii. 1. 159-165
A sweeter and a lovelier ... :	*Richard III*, i. 2. 242-245
the front of Jove himself ... :	*Hamlet*, iii. 4. 56-62
He would not flatter Neptune ... :	*Coriolanus*, iii. 1. 256-257

For his bounty ...:   *Antony and Cleopatra*, v. 2. 86
in bestowing ...:   *Henry VIII*, iv. 2. 56-63
Contempt nor bitterness ...: *All's Well That Ends Well*, i. 2.
                                      36-48

One, in suff'ring all ...:   *Hamlet*, iii. 2. 71-78
Nothing in his life ...:   *Macbeth*, i. 4. 7-11
His overthrow heap'd ...:   *Henry VIII*, iv. 2. 64-68
His life was gentle ...:   *Julius Caesar*, v. 5. 73-75

A MOST IMPERFECT MAN

A slave, whom ...:   *Timon of Athens*, iv. 3. 251-259
He will steal ...:   *All's Well That Ends Well*, iv. 3.
                                    280-292

A stubborn soul ...:   *Measure for Measure*, v. 1. 485-486
An inhuman wretch ...:   *The Merchant of Venice*, iv. 1. 4-6
A notorious liar ...:   *All's Well That Ends Well*, i. 1.
                                    111-112

An hourly promise ...:   *All's Well That Ends Well*, iii. 6.
                                    11

A wretch whom ...:   *King's Lear*, i. 1. 215-216
Such smiling rogues ...:   *King Lear*, ii. 2. 79-86
A knave, a rascal ...:   *King Lear*, ii. 2. 15-23

A PERFECT WOMAN

One woman is fair ...:   *Much Ado About Nothing*, ii. 3.
                                    27-37

Full many a lady ...:   *The Tempest*, iii. 1. 39-48
She's fair and royal ...:   *Cymbeline*, iii. 5. 70-74
The senate house ...:   *Pericles*, i. 1. 10-11
She excels each mortal ...: *Two Gentlemen of Verona*, iv. 2.
                                    51-53

a lady, wiser, fairer ...:   *Troilus and Cressida*, i. 3. 275-276
whose youth ...:   *Troilus and Cressida*, ii. 2. 78-79
with a mind ...:   *Troilus and Cressida*, iii. 2. 169-
                                  170

Why if two gods ...:   *The Merchant of Venice*, iii. 5. 84-
                                  87

Falseness cannot come ...: *Pericles*, v. 1. 121-123

AN IMPERFECT WOMAN

She's the kitchen wench ... :	*Comedy of Errors,* iii. 2. 96-143
She speaks poniards ... :	*Much Ado About Nothing,* ii. 1. 255-269

ANYBODY'S WOMAN

Who is't can read ... :	*Cymbeline,* v. 5. 48
This woman's an easy glove ... :	*All's Well That Ends Well,* v. 3. 278-9
Every inch of woman ... :	*The Winter's Tale,* ii. 1. 137-138
Frailty, thy name ... :	*Hamlet,* i. 2. 146
God hath given you ... :	*Hamlet,* iii. 1. 149-153
He's mad that trusts ... :	*King Lear,* iii. 6. 19-21
You are not oathable ... :	*Timon of Athens,* iv. 3. 135-138
The wiles and guiles ... :	*The Passionate Pilgrim,* xviii. 37-40
Proper deformity seems not ... :	*King Lear,* iv. 2. 60-61
Behold yon simpering ... :	*King Lear,* iv. 6. 120-134
O indistinguished space ... :	*King Lear,* iv. 6. 278
There's no motion ... :	*Cymbeline,* ii. 5. 20-32
What woman in the city ... :	*As You Like It,* ii. 7. 74-76
There's language in her ... :	*Troilus and Cressida,* iv. 5. 55-63

ON VIRGINITY

Are you meditating ... :	*All's Well That Ends Well,* i. 1. 121
It is not politic ... :	*All's Well That Ends Well,* i. 1. 137
Virginity being ... :	*All's Well That Ends Well,* i. 1. 134-135
Loss of virginity ...	*All's Well That Ends Well,* i. 1. 138-145
There's little can ... :	*All's Well That Ends Well,* i. 1. 147-162
'Tis a commodity ... :	*All's Well That Ends Well,* i. 1. 165-178

SOME STRANGE FELLOWS

Nature hath fram'd ... :	*The Merchant of Venice,* i. 1. 51-56
Some men there ... :	*The Merchant of Venice,* iv. 1. 47-52

Who would believe...:	*The Tempest*, iii. 3. 44-47
I knew a man...:	*Two Noble Kinsmen*, v. 1. 107-116
There is the...:	*The Merchant of Venice*, i. 2. 43-96
This one...hath...:	*Troilus and Cressida*, i. 2. 19-31
Faith, here's a...:	*Macbeth*, ii. 3. 9
A gull, a fool...:	*Henry V*, iii. 6. 70-83
[Here's] a servingman, proud...:	*King Lear*, iii. 4. 87-97
The country gives...:	*King Lear*, ii. 3. 13-19
Poor Tom? whom...:	*King Lear*, iii. 4. 51-58
You must learn...:	*Henry V*, iii. 6. 83-85

A COURTIER

Came there a certain...:	*1 Henry IV*, i. 3. 33-64
This fellow pecks up...:	*Love's Labour's Lost*, v. 2. 315-316
A snapper-up of unconsidered...:	*The Winter's Tale*, iv. 3. 26
He is wit's peddlar...:	*Love's Labour's Lost*, v. 2. 317-334
A refined traveller...:	*Love's Labour's Lost*, i. 1. 164-170
He did comply with...:	*Hamlet*, v. 2. 195-202

A BIG TALKER

He speaks an...:	*The Merchant of Venice*, i. 1. 114
he his special nothing...:	*All's Well That Ends Well*, ii. 1. 95
His reasons are...:	*The Merchant of Venice*, i. 1. 115-118
A gentleman...:	*Romeo and Juliet*, ii. 4. 155
Talkers are no...:	*Richard III*, i. 3. 351
Hear him debate...:	*Henry V*, i. 1. 41-52
A good traveller...:	*All's Well That Ends Well*, ii. 5. 30
saving in dialogue...:	*King John*, i. 1. 201
Here's a large mouth...:	*King John*, ii. 1. 458-466
He...talks like a knell...:	*Coriolanus*, v. 4. 22-24

ON WOMAN'S RIGHTS

A woman mov'd...:	*The Taming of the Shrew*, v. 2. 142-160
Why, headstrong liberty...:	*The Comedy of Errors*, ii. 1. 15-24
But it is their husbands'...:	*Othello*, iv. 3. 89-106

YOUTH AND AGE

The satiricial rogue ... :	*Hamlet*, ii. 2. 199-204
Old, cold, wither'd ... :	*The Merry Wives of Windsor*, v. 5. 161
Do you set down ... :	*2 Henry IV*, i. 2. 201-208
When the age ... :	*Much Ado About Nothing*, iii. 5. 37
A good leg will fall ... :	*Henry V*, v. 2. 167-174
The elder I wax ... :	*Henry V*, v. 2. 246-249
Give me always ... :	*2 Henry IV*, iii. 2. 294
I would there were ... :	*The Winter's Tale*, iii. 3. 60
I had rather have ... :	*Cymbeline*, iv. 2. 199
Sons at perfect age ... :	*King Lear*, i. 2. 77-79
The younger rises ... :	*King Lear*, iii. 3. 26
Our own precedent ... :	*Timon of Athens*, i. 1. 134
All's brave that ... :	*As You Like It*, iii. 4. 49
To be fantastic ... :	*Two Gentlemen of Verona*, ii. 7. 47
for youth no less ... :	*Hamlet*, iv. 7. 79-82
Lust and liberty ... :	*Timon of Athens*, iv. 1. 25-28
such wanton, wild, ... :	*Hamlet*, ii. 1. 22-26
in the morn and ... :	*Hamlet*, i. 3. 41-42
By heaven, it is ... :	*Hamlet*, ii. 1. 114
Crabbed age ... :	*The Passionate Pilgrim*, xii. 1-9

A PERFECT HORSE

Let my horse ... :	*Henry V*, iii. 7. 4-43
Imperiously he leaps ... :	*Venus and Adonis*, 265-300

ENGLAND

When Julius ... :	*Cymbeline*, iii. 1. 2-33
In our not-fearing Britain ... :	*Cymbeline*, ii. 4. 19
Our countrymen ... :	*Cymbeline*, ii. 4. 20-26
England breeds ... :	*Henry V*, iii. 7. 150-162
Froissart ... records ... :	*1 Henry VI*, i. 2. 29-36
I' th' world's ... :	*Cymbeline*, iii. 4. 140-142
This royal throne ... :	*Richard II*, ii. 1. 40-63
This England never ... :	*King John*, v. 7. 112-118
O England! model ... :	*Henry V*, ii. prologue. 16-19